C000099899

Rail and Roa~~d Transp...~~
on the Isle of Portland

A Pictorial Survey

by
B.L. Jackson

THE OAKWOOD PRESS

© Oakwood Press & B.L. Jackson 2002
British Library Cataloguing in Publication Data
A Record for this book is available from the British Library
ISBN 0 85361 581 0
Typeset by Oakwood Graphics.
Repro by Ford Graphics, Ringwood, Hants.
Printed by Cambrian Printers Ltd, Aberystwyth, Dyfed.

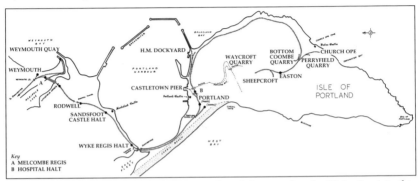

Title page: Rodwell station, towards Weymouth and the tunnel under Wyke Road. In this idyllic rural scene taken prior to the 1907 alterations, it is difficult to imagine that this station lay less than half a mile from Weymouth's town centre serving the Chapelhay and Rodwell districts. Opened in 1870 it was the second station to open within the Borough.
Dorset County Museum

Front cover, top: Ivatt class '2' 2-6-2 tank No. 41284 departs from Portland for Weymouth with the last-ever passenger train on Saturday 27th March, 1965. Behind, and 490 ft above, stands the Verne Citadel, and a scar on the hillside marks the course of the Merchants' Railway of 1825, Portland's first railway. One hundred and forty years later the final chapter comes to a close.
J.W.T. House/C.L. Caddy Collection

Front cover, bottom: Photographed at Bincleaves Road, Weymouth on 10th August, 1969, Bristol LSW6B No. 1852, LTA 995, is hard at work conveying passengers to Portland Navy days. The ECW L27/28R body had staggered seats on the upper deck. When new in 1953 this vehicle had been regularly employed on the Weymouth-Salisbury service (a round trip of 100 miles). She was withdrawn in 1971, passing through two independent operators before preservation in 1975. Today, No. 1852 resides at the Haynes Motor Museum, Sparkford, Somerset.
D.M. Habgood

Rear cover, top: Pannier tank Nos. 4624 stands at Easton station on Sunday 8th July, 1956 whilst working the Railway Travel & Correspondence Society 'Wessex Wyvern' special that toured various Dorset branch lines. The train consisted of former LSWR three-coach non-corridor set No. 163, a feature of these sets being the sliding door to the luggage compartment in the guard's van. Easton engine shed to the left had already been demolished, although the water tower remained still in the light stone livery of the GWR.
Colour Rail

Rear cover, bottom: Dennis Dart SLF No. 827, T827 AFX, with Plaxton Pointer II N39F bodywork, waits to depart from the King's Statue for Littlemoor estate in June 2001, painted in the First Group 'Barbie' livery, with the blue route branding for Littlemoor above the windows. From November 2001 'Southern National' was dropped from the fleet name, and as this book goes to press it was announced that the 'Metro' is to be replaced by 'Overground'.
Author

Published by The Oakwood Press (Usk), P.O. Box 13, Usk, Mon., NP15 1YS.
E-mail: oakwood-press@dial.pipex.com
Website: www.oakwood-press.dial.pipex.com

Contents

Priory Corner photographed around the turn of the 19th century. To the right is a Burrell double-crank compound traction engine bringing two trailers of stone from the quarries. In the foreground a Burrell single-crank compound stands by, whilst on the left stone is transferred to a Merchants' Railway wagon by the crane as a team of horses returns with empty wagons. *Author's Collection*

Seven Bristol VRTs lined up at Edward Street depot before their day's work early in the morning of 2nd May 1974. *Left to right*, Nos. 1075, BFJ 175L; 1066, ATA 166L; 1072, BFJ 172L; 1067, ATA 167L; 1073, BFJ 173L; 1052, OTA 286G and 1074, BFJ 174L. No. 1075 has in recent years been acquired for private preservation. *Author*

Acknowledgements

Many people have assisted in the writing of this work, sometimes quite unwittingly by supplying a snippet of information that has helped to complete the complex history contained in the four volumes recording the story of the Isle of Portland railways and associated bus services.

Special thanks to Messrs M.S. Curtis, R. Grimley, D. Persson, L. Ronan, and B. Thirlwall for their assistance in updating the bus services, George Pryer for overseeing the complete proof reading of the work and his expert assistance on railway matters, and also Maureen Attwooll, R.J. Crawley, P. Legg, and R.C. Riley.

The copyright of the various photographers is acknowledged alongside the captions to the photographs.

Over the years taken by the research for this series it is regretted that many older enthusiasts, railwaymen, and busmen have taken their final journey without seeing the completed work. Therefore this work is dedicated to them, and indeed to all who have been involved in transport in the Weymouth and Portland area over the years.

Special thanks go to the Oakwood team for their enthusiasm, assistance and support during of the production of this series. Finally I should like to thank my wife, herself a Portlander, for her encouragement and help without which these works could not have been written.

A 1930s view of the Backwater viaduct, with an 'O2' on a four-coach 'Gate Set' heading off the viaduct towards Melcombe Regis station. In the foreground people are engaged in the age-old custom of feeding the swans from the end of Radipole Park Drive.

Author's Collection

Introduction

The existing trilogy of the *Isle of Portland Railways* books by the same author (published by Oakwood Press) had covered most of the history of transport facilities in the area, but there are practical and economic limitations to the contents of any one volume and there remains a fund of unpublished material - mainly photographs - which is nevertheless of considerable interest. Even after years of research there is always the picture or obscure fact that emerges after publication, and whilst nobody has produced any real gem - such as the first train to Easton or wartime traffic on the branch - several other fascinating photographs have come to light.

Furthermore, whilst Volume Two of the trilogy was able to cover the entire railway history from early plans to the present day (well after closure), leaving little to be added to the already printed word, the story of the associated bus services is somewhat different. Indeed this has become even more complicated since 1969, at which point Volume Three ended, and there have been many changes in the last 20 years - some of them so rapid as to escape the attention of all but the keenest observer! It has therefore been necessary to update the bus history to the latter part of 2001, but it must be remembered that the story is an ongoing one and changes are taking place all the time.

The publication of this work, originally conceived as a purely photographic album, coincides with the 50th anniversary of the closure of the Portland branch to passengers in March 1952 and the centenary of the opening of the Easton section to passenger traffic in 1902, and is therefore a very appropriate time to bring the story to a close.

I am coming home from PORTLAND

Mothers'-in-law and railways have been the subject of music hall jokes and material for comic postcards for many years. This fine example of a gentleman walking home from Portland is no exception. *Maureen Attwooll Collection*

An early view of activities at Priory Corner, a team of horses having arrived with a wagon loaded with stone from the quarries, which will now be transferred by the crane. In the background are clear signs of where recent work has taken place in the construction of the Verne Citadel. *Author's Collection*

Loading stone onto a Merchants' Railway wagon at Priory Corner. To the right, behind the crane jib are the rear wheels of one of the six-wheel Sentinel steam lorries, this vehicle having brought the stone from the quarry. *The late E. Latcham Collection*

The Merchants' Railway

The Portland Railway (commonly known as the 'Merchants' Railway') was conceived solely for the transport of stone. In 1824 plans were drawn up for its construction to run along a ledge on the north side of the Island, eastwards from a point known as Priory Corner to curve around the edge of what is now the base of the earthworks of the Verne Fort, from where it would descend to sea level at a point near Portland Castle by means of a 586 yds-long inclined plain. Unlike many early tramways and industrial railways of the period, the proprietors went to Parliament to obtain an Act for the construction of the line, this being obtained on the 10th June, 1825, thus making it a public company. Construction went ahead quickly, and it was opened to traffic by October 1826. In the short period between then and 31st December that year 4,803 tons of stone were carried over the line

The stone was brought to Priory Corner from the quarries in horse-drawn carts and transferred by crane at that point onto 4 ft 6 in. gauge wagons, and then hitched to a team of horses which proceeded to haul them along the hillside ledge and around the side of Verne Hill to the top drum of the incline. This was situated just below a point where the road to the north entrance of the present Verne Prison crossed the line on a bridge, the second drum being situated half-way down the incline.

On reaching the top drum the horses were unhitched and the wagons lowered down the first incline on the end of a chain wound several times around the drum. Speed was controlled by the weight of empty wagons being hauled up on the other end of the chain. A brake on the drum assisted control. This process was repeated for the second stage of the journey. Quarry owners subsequently laid private lines from Priory Corner into their quarries on the west side of the Island, and at various times short inclines were constructed from the quarries at Yeates to meet the company's line.

Owing to construction work taking place in connection with the Verne fortifications during the 1860s, the short incline which ran down from what later become the Verne's South Gate to the main line at the head of Tillycombe was removed. In its reconstructed form it became the incline running from New Ground down under the three bridges to the main line. In 1860 it was decided to alter the two brake drum systems on the main incline, and one drum was installed to control the entire descent.

With the opening of the Weymouth & Portland Railway in 1865 a short branch from Portland station to Castletown enabled exchange sidings to be established at the foot of the incline, allowing stone to be transferred to the main line system. Traffic on the railway increased so rapidly thereafter that it was decided to double part of the line from the top of the incline to cater for the expanding trade.

By 1894 the lease on land at Castletown was running out. As about half the tonnage carried by the railway was shipped from the piers urgent action was necessary to protect the company's interest, resulting in the construction of a new pier to the east of the previous site. Work commenced in August 1897 and was completed in December 1898. It necessitated laying an additional section of line which, after crossing Castle Road, turned right and then ran alongside it for about 100 yards before bearing left onto the pier. In the last 10 years of the 19th

A Victorian view looking up the incline under the three arches from Tillycombe. The arch rising at an angle carries the road from Fortuneswell to the south gate of the Verne, whilst the arch above it carries the upper level of the Merchants' Railway. Mostly concealed behind this is the top arch carrying the road across New Ground to the south gate of the Verne, through which can be seen the incline brake drum. *Author's Collection*

One loaded and one empty wagon descending the Merchants' Railway incline. Clearly shown are the rollers set in their pedestals that guide the haulage wire. Note the use of just three rails, the centre rail being common except at the halfway passing point where a conventional loop existed. The crude yet practical construction of the wagons is of note. To this day many of the wheels are in use as sinkers for small boat moorings in the area. *A. Hutchings Collection*

century, 890,888 tons of stone left the Island by way of the Merchants' Railway, the highest figure of 63,315 tons during 1899 and the lowest, 32,346 tons during 1895.

Between 1900 and the end of 1914, 842,152 tons of stone had been carried over the line. The last ship to call before war was declared carried the largest consignment to date - 530 tons. The subsequent decline in traffic caused the railway to close in June 1917, remaining so until January 1920. The feeder branches were removed, leaving only the main line from Priory Corner to Castletown. Although the Easton & Church Hope Railway and the traction engine had caused inroads into trade, the introduction of the motor lorry and the changing world were to influence the final years. However, with its direct connection to Castletown pier it was still the best method to transport stone that was departing by sea, and as late as 1937, 400 tons were loaded into one vessel alone.

World War II closed the railway on 11th October, 1939, and it was never to re-open. This was the end of the Portland Railway Company as an operating concern. It had survived into a mechanical age almost certainly because of its cheapness of operation and its usefulness can be measured by the fact that during its working life it is estimated to have carried a total of 4,561,796 tons of stone.

The affairs of the company were eventually wound up in the late 1950s, the rails having been lifted for scrap. Today the earthworks around the Verne are still clearly visible, as is part of the incline. The remainder has returned to nature, or like Priory Corner, vanished with the changing face of the island. Although now used for other purposes Castletown pier remains, a monument to the railway's past.

The Merchants' Railway incline viewed from Castletown, with loaded wagons awaiting forwarding to either the transfer sidings or Castletown pier. In the background is the bridge carrying the railway to the Dockyard and Easton, and the footbridge to the Naval Hospital. *The late E. Latcham Collection*

Castletown pier prior to the 1897 improvements fully described in Volume One. A paddle steamer has just departed from the projecting steamer pier to the right, another short pier to the right is just visible behind the ship's masts. Although some stone was loaded at this point the majority was handled at the old piers, the cranes of which are to the extreme left.

Dorset County Museum

Castletown pier, looking southwards. In the foreground is a discarded ship's anchor and other quayside paraphernalia. To the right wagons of stone from the Merchants' Railway are awaiting shipment, and in the background is a traction engine and trailer. Behind it are the public houses and other buildings of Castletown, whilst high above to the left is the north gate of the Verne Citadel.

Author's Collection

The remains of one of the former spoil tipping points along West Cliff. The wagons were propelled to the edge of the bridge over the track below and the spoil deposited over the cliff.
A. Hutchings Collection

The top of the Merchants' Railway incline as viewed in 1959. The stone rubble on the left is all that remains of the brake drum and other buildings. The steel bridge in the background carried the road to the north entrance of the Verne and has since been replaced by a smaller stone structure.   *Author*

The only known 2 ft gauge steam locomotive on the island was *Excelsior*, an 0-4-2 wing tank built by Bagnall in 1888. Originally used on a private estate railway in Wales, and later assisting in the construction of the Lynton & Barnstaple Light Railway, *Excelsior* was purchased by Messrs Barnes of Portland in 1898 and used to remove spoil to be tipped over West Cliff.

E.G. Hoskins Collection

A view of the workings with the top spoil being removed. The 2 ft gauge track and wagons are to the right of the photograph. *E.G. Hoskins Collection*

A former section of quarry railway rail, which now forms a lintel in the Sugarloaf Café, Easton Square, Portland. *Author*

The disused tunnel under Park Road, Easton, where once a tramway connected Park Quarry and Bottom Coombe Quarry. *Author*

Quarrymen stand around a steam crane in an unidentified quarry. Judging by the rudimentary arrangements this could well be one of the original hand-operated cranes that was converted to steam operation around the turn of the century. *E.G. Hoskins Collection*

Amongst the many assorted steam-driven machines used in the stone industry was this rail-mounted travelling crane employed in the masonry yard at Bottom Coombe. Several cranes of this type were purchased from contractors following completion of dockyard contracts. Between the yard and the houses in the background the branch line to Easton crossed the scene, one of the signals being visible. *Author's Collection*

Wagons being loaded in the sidings at Bottom Coombe Masonry Works.   *Author's Collection*

A scene in the South Western Stone Company's quarry at Perryfield. Alongside the quarry in the background are both GWR and LNER wagons awaiting loading.   *Author's Collection*

Bogie bolster wagons were not normally used for the conveyance of stone traffic, but this photograph proves the exception to the rule, and also shows one of the bogies derailed on pointwork in Perryfield Siding. No doubt the onlookers are discussing a way to rectify the matter quickly and quietly. *Author's Collection*

Once used by the stone firms for moving wagons in their sidings and now preserved is this 'BSA Truck Mover', a machine of lawnmower-like appearance powered by a 420 cc side valve engine capable of moving 75 tons. The grooved wheel is run along the rail until under the end of the wagon, a hydraulic ram is then brought into contact with the wagon chassis, thus securely locking the truck mover between the rail and wagon, the clutch is then engaged and the trucks moved to where required. *Author*

Road Locomotives

As fully described in Volume One of *Isle of Portland Railways*, the traction engines and later steam lorries were inextricably involved with the railway scene by reason of their work in the haulage of stone between quarries, the stone mills and the railheads. A further selection of photographs is offered here, including several early engines.

Burrell single-crank compound No. 2060, new in December 1897 to J. Pearce, stands alongside the Sawmill Tavern in Easton Lane, before proceeding into the sawmills. Note how the long block of stone was carried, supported by the two primitive trailers. No. 2060 was the only single-crank compound engine on the island engaged in the stone trade, and was sold in 1898. *Author's Collection*

Burrell double-crank compound No. 2083, new to J. Lano & Sons of Portland in May 1898, poses in Easton Square. Fitted with a long canopy and small belly tank, this locomotive passed to the Bath & Portland Stone Firms in 1913. In 1917 it was sold to Lott & Walne of Dorchester and was later acquired by Miller & Sons of Bristol, converted to Showmen's specification and named *Marshal Foch*, later passing to Jennings Bros of Devizes. *Author's Collection*

Portland. Fortunes Well and General View.

In this pre-1914 view an unidentified Fowler of F.J. Barnes turns into the top of Fortuneswell, before the steep descent to Victoria Square. The buildings on the left-hand side of the corner in the foreground, known as 'Antediluvian Cottage' and 'Yew Tree House', were demolished to make way for the construction of the new Portland Urban District Council offices in 1933.

Author's Collection

Burrell double-crank compound No. 2549, FX 6684, draws a wagon load of spoil out of a quarry. New to J. Lano & Sons in 1903 and passing to the Bath & Portland Stone Firms in 1913, she remained in service until 1932.

Author's Collection

Set against a background of Fortuneswell and the Chesil Beach, two unidentified Burrell double-crank compound engines stand at Priory Corner. The load from the leading trailer of the left-hand engine has already been transferred by crane onto the Merchants' Railway, and workmen are about to commence unloading the second trailer.   *Author's Collection*

The scene at the bottom of Verne Common Road following the runaway of Fowler No. 8839, FX 6660, *Sphinx* on 25th July, 1921, which caused fatal injuries to the steersman, George White. The details of the wagon used to convey the stone and the methods of securing the load are clearly shown.   *Author's Collection*

Photographed climbing Easton Lane with two well-loaded wagons in tow is Burrell double-crank compound No. 3980 (PR 2474), new in 1924 to Bath & Portland Stone Firms Ltd. Sold in 1932 this road locomotive was converted to Showmen's specification for Charles Heal of Glastonbury and named *Her Majesty*, ending her working life with Armstrong of Nottingham in 1954.   *Author's Collection*

One of the Sentinel DG6 steam waggons employed by Messrs Newman & Masters of Lytchett Minster for hauling rubble from Portland for the construction of Westwey Road at Weymouth, is here viewed loading at quarries opposite Perryfield House.   *Author's Collection*

Sentinel DG6 steam waggons Nos. 8026 and 8027, TK 3336 and TK 3337, depositing stone during the construction of Westwey Road. Clearly demonstrated in the photograph is the three-way tipping arrangement of the 200 cubic feet bodies. Both waggons were new in August 1929, each costing £1,350, but the advances in both the petrol and diesel lorry and a sharp increase in road tax for steam driven vehicles soon put them off the road. *Author's Collection*

The first two steam waggons purchased by F.J. Barnes Ltd in December 1931 are photographed before departure from the Sentinel works at Shrewsbury. They are DG4 models. On the right No. 8619, fleet No. 1, TK 7082, with No. 8620, No. 2, TK 7083, to the left. *Author's Collection*

Bath & Portland Stone Firms Sentinel DG6 No. 8687, fleet No. 3, TK 7674, photographed upon delivery to Portland in April 1932. *J. Ritchie Collection*

The successor to the traction engine and steam lorry was the AEC Mammoth Major eight-wheel lorry, the answer to the stone haulage problem. Versatile and reliable, Bath & Portland Stone Firms ran a fleet of these and the four-wheel AEC Monarch. Well maintained, they served well. This example JT 7154 was new in 1937 and survived until 1967 when broken up by a local scrap merchant. *Author*

An illustration showing construction of the breakwater, with the inclines and work around the Verne in the background, whilst in the foreground is the open timber structure allowing wagons to dump stone into the sea and build up the breakwater itself. To the far left a Mitchell screw pile is being placed to enable an extension of the platform structure to be made.

S. Morris Collection

Photographs of the original broad gauge locomotives used during the construction of the breakwater are almost non-existent. Once their work at Portland was completed they passed to other owners, No. 454 along with other equipment going to the Isle of Man for use in the construction of Port Erin breakwater. Named *Henry B. Loch*, No. 454 is shown with wagons in an adjacent quarry.

Manx National Heritage

The Breakwater and Dockyard Railway

The harbour and associated works at Portland resulted from the invasion fears of the 19th century, when the 'Palmerston' Defence Works were erected around the shores of Southern England. The work, which was originally intended to be simply a breakwater, quickly developed into a massive defence system to protect the Weymouth and Portland area. The projects involved were a fort on the north side of Portland (on top of Verne Hill) protected by a dry moat, gun emplacements at East Weares, a fort on the end of the breakwater (later known as Chequered Fort), the Nothe Fort at the entrance to Weymouth Harbour, and Upton Fort at Osmington Mills on the east side of Weymouth Bay. In August 1848 construction was started of the gravity - operated railway from the Grove to the north-east corner of the island situated 400 ft below, from which point the breakwater was to commence. A temporary prison to house the convicts who were to be employed on quarry work was constructed, the first convicts having arrived in November 1848.

The railway consisted of three separate inclines each 1,500 ft long, in line with each other on a gradient varying from 1 in 10 to 1 in 15. At the top of each incline there was an overhead brake drum fitted with a powerful screw brake controlling the cable for each section. Loaded descending wagons hauled the empty ones up on two separate 7 ft broad gauge railway tracks. There was also a separate incline at right angles to serve the Verne moat.

Work on the breakwater commenced in 1849, the foundation stone being dropped onto the seabed by Prince Albert, the Prince Consort, on 25th July, 1849. To enable the breakwater to be built substantial timber staging was erected on piles, some up to 120 ft long, and railway tracks were laid along the top which had no decking. Wagons were propelled to the required position to allow the stone to drop through a trap door in the floor of the wagon into the sea below. Derailments and accidents were commonplace, at times causing death or injury. Twenty-two men died in accidents and five others were drowned.

Initially horses were used to haul the wagons onto the staging until the summer of 1851 when the first steam locomotive commenced work. Later three new 0-4-0 well tank locomotives built by Wilson of Leeds arrived. Of the five locomotives recorded at Portland at least two survived for further work, *Queen* ending her days on the Torbay & Brixham Railway, and No. 454 went to Port Erin on the Isle of Man, where she was again employed on breakwater construction.

The original Portland breakwater, consisting of two arms, was completed on 4th March, 1871. On 18th August, 1872 the Prince of Wales (later King Edward VII) arrived at Portland to declare the project complete. It is estimated that nearly six million tons of stone went into its construction.

As the breakwater and harbour works developed it was desirable to form a link with the Weymouth & Portland Railway, and an Act of Parliament was obtained in 1871 for the construction of a line from Castletown to the breakwater. Work commenced on 28th July, 1874. Much of the broad gauge line on the breakwater works was relaid as standard gauge, where possible the existing rails being reused, and construction was completed in February 1876, although the line was not open to traffic until early 1878. No locomotives were involved, wagons on the goods-only line being hauled by horses.

Bagnall No. 1496 (No. 4) photographed at the builder's works in Stafford before delivery in February 1897. With the background details obliterated, copies of this photograph were used by the company for publicity purposes. *Allen Civil Collection*

No. 1496 (No. 4) photographed at Hamworthy Quay. Following her sale from Portland Dockyard to J. Smith of Hamworthy, Poole, in 1925 she was resold to the Hamworthy Wharf & Coal Company, and named *Iris*. Under various owners she survived until scrapped in 1950.

Great Western Trust

The development of the torpedo had undermined the effiency of the original defence works, ships at anchor in the roads now being sitting targets in the event of an attack. To protect the harbour two new 'Defensive Breakwaters' were constructed to enclose the two-mile gap between the Breakwater Fort and Bincleaves on the Weymouth side. The method of constructing the new breakwaters was to differ from the old. Stone was brought down to the Dockyard where it was loaded into special barges which were towed to the site for unloading, either through bottom doors onto the sea-bed, or in the case of large blocks above sea level, lifted off by crane.

Work commenced in 1894 using direct labour together with convict labour in the quarries. Three years later the work was handed over to Messrs Hill & Company, but convict labour was retained in the quarries and work progressed rapidly. By the middle of April 1899 the new work had been raised to low water level, although work continued for several years in building up the breakwater before it was complete. Other work was carried out to improve the shore establishments. The coaling facilities were extended and the first of the oil tanks installed for what was to become the fuel of the future.

The engines used on the project were the latest available from engine builders, the first four Bagnall 0-4-0 saddle tanks arriving in late 1896/early 1897, with two Peckett 0-4-0 and one 0-6-0 saddle tank being delivered during 1898. Several second-hand engines were added, in all nine locomotives being employed by the turn of the century. Some of the original engines were disposed of over the years and an Andrew Barclay 0-4-0 saddle tank was added in 1917, this being the last to survive in service.

Over the years there was always a small amount of stone required to top up the breakwater and the incline and the quarry lines remained in occasional use, an engine being kept in the engine shed at the top of the incline for the purpose. In 1921 the prison became a Borstal Institution. It was considered that quarry work was unsuitable for Borstal boys, but a small amount of stone was removed by direct labour until the mid-1930s after which the stone companies supplied material for this work which included delivery to the Dockyard. The Admiralty quarry closed, the engine being brought down from the top and the rails and brake drums removed from the incline. The remainder of the Dockyard railway continued to operate carrying the stores and equipment required by the Navy

In December 1960 two Fowler 0-4-0 diesel shunters arrived at Portland. The end was now fast approaching for steam, the last survivor being in steam during Navy Days at Whitsun 1961 when, wearing the traditional long funnel and other decorations, she gave rides in an open wagon along part of the breakwater railway. She then lay out of use until January 1963 when she was transported to a scrapyard to be broken up. The two diesels were active until the closure of the Portland branch in April 1965 after which they lay idle until 1967 when they were sold, thus ending the story of railways on Portland Breakwater and Dockyard.

A much greater project than originally envisaged, the completed works formed the largest man-made harbour in the world, and were soon to prove their worth with the onset of World War I. After the uncertainties of the 1920s and 1930s, Portland came into its own in 1939 with the outbreak of another war.

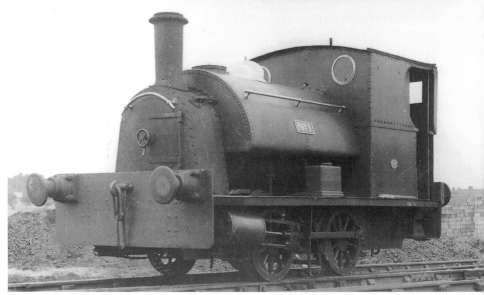

Bagnall No. 1493 (No. 3) remained at Portland until sold to J. Smith of Hamworthy in 1925. Resold to The Hastings & St Leonards Gas Company and renumbered No. 1, she worked at the Glydne Gas Works where she was photographed in August 1951. She was broken up on site by Messrs Cohen in June 1954. *John H. Meredith*

George Caddy driving one of the two Green-Bat 2 ft gauge battery electric locomotives used at Bincleaves. The event is a ceremonial send off for the gentleman riding the decorated torpedo! Behind lie four of the former German patrol boats put to use as torpedo recovery vessels for the testing establishment in the background. *A. Hengst*

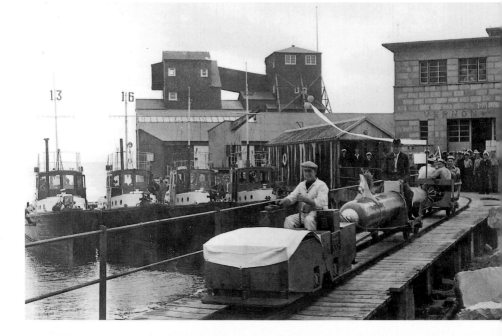

Many clandestine cross-channel operations were carried out from Portland, and the harbour played a vital part in the build up to D-Day and the ending of the war.

When peace returned the harbour again became the base for the home fleet and training squadrons, but reductions in the fleet resulted in Dockyard facilities being pruned towards the end of the 1950s, at which time the Royal Naval helicopter station was opened. The submarine training squadron moved away, and it was not until the Falklands conflict of 1982 that Portland was again able to prove its worth in times of crisis, but by that time it was not served by a railway.

In recent years the whole Dockyard and the other defence establishments on the island have closed, and under the name of 'Portland Port' the facilities and harbour are now a commercial undertaking. The great naval fleet, like the activities of the Dockyard and its railway, are fading memories.

Peckett No. 987 of 1898 survived at Portland Dockyard for her entire working life until scrapped in 1959. Photographed here in full regalia for Portland Navy Days when rides would be given to the general public in open wagons through the dockyard and out onto the inner part of the breakwater, technically the only occasions a passenger service operated on the Breakwater Railway!   *D. Hawkins*

Right: Pannier tanks Nos. 3737 and 4624 wait to depart from the dockyard with the Royal Train on 29th April, 1959 following a visit by Her Majesty the Queen and HRH Prince Charles. *Colour Rail/S.C. Townroe*

Below: One of the many postcard views available around the turn of the century depicting convicts at work in the Admiralty quarries. In the background the railway lines and wagons can be seen. *Author's Collection*

Bottom: The block stacking yard near the convict prison, which can be seen in the background. As well as supplying the Portland project, stone was dispatched around the country to other Government projects. *W. Macey Collection*

A Dockyard Railway wagon, having been propelled along the loading jetty, is lifted by steam crane allowing its contents to be tipped into a barge for transfer to the breakwater extension works. *W. Macey Collection*

Work in progress during 1907 on the reconstruction of the viaduct connecting the railway on the breakwater with the coal store on 'Monkey Island' which was situated behind the cameraman. *W. Macey Collection*

An interior view of the Verne Citadel taken during 1877. The two blocks of bachelor officers' quarters are to the fore. Behind the block on the left can be seen the top of the sergeants' mess. Apart from the left-hand accommodation block, which was bombed during World War II, all the other buildings in the photograph now form part of the Verne prison complex. The curved railway track across the bottom of the picture is evidence of the line used during the Verne's construction.   *Royal Engineers Library Chatham*

With the U-boat threat a seaplane base was established at Portland during World War I. Before a hanger was constructed the primitive arrangements shown here were brought into use. The Easton line and the entrance to the dockyard system are at the bottom of the photograph, whilst the remains of the tracks formerly leading to the stone-loading jetty are to the left. Camber jetty occupies the right of the photograph.   *Author's Collection*

The breakwater viewed from the Bincleaves end shortly after completion of the initial work, much of which was carried out by the Great Western Railway with the intention of constructing docks for their Channel Islands traffic in Newtons Cove, to the left. The scheme was abandoned during the early 1900s and the site taken over by the Admiralty, who constructed the torpedo testing establishment on the arm protruding into the Portland harbour. Later a large area of the landward site was reclaimed and a larger torpedo establishment erected. Ironically today it is the only Admiralty establishment surviving in the area as 'QinetiQ', a company wholly owned by the Ministry of Defence. *Author's Collection*

A wartime view of Portland Dockyard. The Easton & Church Hope Railway can be seen running between the dockyard and the Verne before curving and winding its way around the east side of the Island. The course of the three inclines of the former Admiralty Incline after passing under the Easton line climbs towards Grove. In the foreground is the end of the breakwater, 'Monkey Island' and other dockyard buildings, the coaling pier being at the bottom of the picture. *Crown Copyright*

According to an authoratitive account in the *Railway Magazine* of 1909, amongst the early LSWR four-wheel coaches used on the branch was reputed to be a former Royal saloon constructed in 1851 for the use of Queen Victoria's children. Following its later use as a 1st class saloon it was sold to the Plymouth, Devonport & South Western Junction Railway, and by 1910 to the Kent & East Sussex Light Railway where this photograph was taken in 1933. In 1936 it was sold to a Sussex farmer and survived until the early 1960s.   *Oakwood Picture Library Collection*

A pre-war view, looking towards Weymouth station. In the foreground class 'O2' No. 221 stands on the 'down shed road', whilst a GWR 'Hall' class shunts across the 'up shed road' to gain access to the station. In the background a 'Dean Goods' is engaged on pilot duty, and in the right background is Weymouth Junction signal box with the up and down 'Portland branch loops' behind it.   *Lens of Sutton*

The Portland Branch

The first main line railway arrived in Dorset on 1st June, 1847 when the Southampton & Dorchester Railway reached the County Town. It was to be a further 10 years before the Wilts, Somerset & Weymouth Railway reached Weymouth via Frome, Yeovil and Dorchester, from a junction with the GWR London-Bristol line near Chippenham, the first train running to Weymouth on 20th January, 1857, by which time both lines had been absorbed into their parent systems; the Southampton & Dorchester into the LSWR, and the Wilts, Somerset & Weymouth, into the GWR. As the LSWR was standard gauge and the GWR broad gauge, it resulted in the section between Dorchester Junction and Weymouth being of mixed gauge construction.

From that time there were plans for a railway to Portland, the prospect of a highly lucrative stone traffic being the main consideration. However, it was not until 1861 that a satisfactory scheme was decided upon and the Weymouth & Portland Railway Company was formed, receiving the Royal Assent on 30th June, 1862. It was agreed that the LSWR and the GWR would jointly work the line on behalf of the local company.

Construction commenced in December 1862 and proceeded well, the work being completed by May 1864 when a Board of Trade inspection was carried out. Unfortunately the Inspector insisted on improvements particularly to the viaducts over the Backwater at Weymouth and the Fleet at Wyke Regis, but these problems faded into insignificance compared with the disagreements between the operating companies over working arrangements. The matter went to arbitration before the completed line eventually opened on 16th October, 1865. In June 1870 an intermediate station was opened at Rodwell on the south side of Weymouth.

As with the main line between Dorchester and Weymouth the branch was also laid with mixed gauge. The LSWR ran the entire passenger service, the GWR only participating in its share of the goods traffic. June 1874 saw the broad gauge abolished on the Wilts, Somerset & Weymouth section of the GWR, and shortly afterwards the GWR took over its share of branch passenger working, usually on a yearly basis.

In 1867 the Easton & Church Hope Railway obtained an Act of Parliament to construct a line from quarries north of Easton via an incline to a pier at the base of cliffs near Church Ope Cove on the east side. But the exposed position of the proposed pier and the established Merchants' Railway killed enthusiasm for the scheme. The company then decided to build a steeply graded line around the east side of the island, obtaining running rights over the Admiralty Railway to reach the Weymouth & Portland Railway at Castletown. Many setbacks, extra Acts of Parliament and extensions of time were required before the line was completed in October 1900, when it failed the Board of Trade inspection. It only opened for goods traffic until remedial work was carried out and passenger services commenced on 1st September, 1902. The extension resulted in a temporary station at Portland to accommodate the Easton trains until a new station was completed in May 1905. Other improvements included reconstructed viaducts at the Fleet and over the Backwater at Weymouth in 1902 and 1909, the rebuilding of Rodwell with a passing loop in 1907, a new station at Melcombe Regis and halts at Westham and Wyke Regis in 1909.

In the early years the LSWR used its diminutive 2-4-0 well tanks for both goods and passenger services, these giving way to the 'O2' class 0-4-4 tanks

A pre-war view of Weymouth Junction signal box from the main line side. The wooden hut and 'pagoda' disappeared following an air raid on the station on 4th May, 1941, the signal box also receiving severe damage.   *Author's Collection*

'O2' No. 223 runs around the Portland branch train at Weymouth Junction. In this pre-war view only the original Jubilee Sidings are shown upon which stand loco coal wagons and covered vans for the Channel Islands fruit trade.   *Lens of Sutton*

after their introduction in 1889, to become the LSWR (and later SR) branch engine until closure to passenger traffic. For a short period between 1907-1912 both LSWR steam railmotors and 'C14' 2-2-0 tanks working push-pull trailers were employed, but both being unsuccessful the work reverted to the 'O2' tanks. Following reconstruction of the viaducts, 'T9' and 'K10' 4-4-0 classes often worked special trains as did the 'A12' 'Jubilee' 0-4-2 locomotives. In later years, 'Q', 'Q1' and 'U' classes were sometimes employed on such duties.

The GWR had used its broad gauge 0-6-0 goods engines prior to the gauge conversion, after which various 0-6-0 saddle tanks appeared, the '850' class being followed by the '2021' class. Later the '655' class, having been rebuilt as pannier tanks, worked the branch until replaced by '57XX' pannier tanks. Again, heavier trains were worked by 'Dean Goods' and '2251' class 0-6-0s and '43XX' 2-6-0 locomotives. With the demise of the pannier tanks the branch towards the end was worked by Ivatt class '2MT' 2-6-2 tanks.

As with many branch lines the passenger stock employed in the early days was a motley collection, usually consisting of vintage four-wheelers 'cascaded' from main line use. The introduction of the steam railmotors and the trailer sets provided the public with a standard of comfort never before experienced on the island. The trailer cars, with their centre entrance protected by iron gates, were synonymous with the branch until 4th May, 1941 when an air raid at Weymouth Junction destroyed the vehicles. Following their loss assorted stock appeared for a while, but by the end of 1944 the regular trains consisted of two LSWR four-coach corridor sets, later reduced to three coaches. Within a short while both of these sets were replaced by GWR stock, trains usually consisting of three coaches and sometimes a luggage van, later reduced to a two-coach train.

For the final 14 months of passenger operation two articulated two-coach sets transferred from the Isle of Sheppey Light Railway formed the regular train sets. Until 1924 these coaches had formed the carriage section of South Eastern & Chatham Railway steam railcars. Not well suited to the Portland branch, their limited brake van capacity required each set to be marshalled with a luggage van and their small low-backed seats were not of the greatest comfort. They were not vestibuled, the only entrances being inward-opening doors at the ends.

Following World War I the branch came under competition from motor bus services, and as these improved they had a severe effect on passenger numbers. Sandsfoot Castle Halt opened in August 1932 to provide access to the tourist attraction and later the housing estate developing nearby. Ironically the outbreak of war in September 1939 was to see the branch worked to capacity, and because of its strategic position it suffered the attention of the Luftwaffe on many occasions. The most serious incidents were the destruction of Portland signal box and damage to the station on 11th August, 1940, and the destruction of Rodwell station building in April 1941.

The alternative bus service, which in many cases was more convenient, affected the branch again in the years following the war and resulted in passenger services being withdrawn from 3rd March, 1952. Goods traffic at that time was still heavy, the stone industry and the Dockyard being the main customers, but this was later to decline and the Beeching plan sealed its fate. On 9th March, 1965 the last freight train ran from the island.

The Weymouth end of the original Backwater viaduct. In this pre-1909 view the edge of the seawall stretching away towards Radipole is clearly shown. Infilling in later years created Jubilee Sidings, Radipole Park Gardens, and Radipole Park Drive. In the centre is Weymouth Junction signal box and the myriad of signals controlling the station and approaches.

Author's Collection

The original Backwater viaduct, looking towards Weymouth station. To the right is Commercial Road and the track of the Weymouth Harbour Tramway, beyond which part of Weymouth goods shed is clearly shown. This section of the old viaduct later (1909) formed the approach road and site of Melcombe Regis station, the area in the foreground being reclaimed to form Melcombe Regis Gardens.

Author's Collection

Following closure and removal of the track the section between the oil tanks and the east side of the Dockyard reverted to the Crown, and was absorbed into the Dockyard complex. The coastal section towards Easton can still be viewed as a scar on the island's east cliffs, whilst sections around Easton have either been filled in or built upon.

At Weymouth, a unique situation for a former urban railway exists. No building has taken place, the track bed between Westham Halt and the Fleet at Ferrybridge is now a footpath and cycle track under the name of the 'Rodwell Trail', and as one walks through Rodwell cutting it is clear to see nature gradually reclaiming over 100 years of history.

Above: Former Burry Port & Gwendreath Valley Railway 0-6-0 saddle tank No. 2194 *Kidwelly* hauls a pre-war up Channel Islands Boat Express across the junction of King Street and Commercial Road. The approach road to Melcombe Regis station is behind the cameraman to the right. Although technically the Weymouth Harbour Tramway was part of the Weymouth & Portland Railway, it was worked as an entirely separate entity. On the corner stood the 'Portland Railway Hotel', already licensed premises when taken over by Messrs Hall & Woodhouse in 1898, and in whose ownership it remained until 1988 when it became a free house, before being converted into private accommodation *Lens of Sutton*
Right: During later years the sign above the door depicted No. 4472 *Flying Scotsman*, a most inept illustration to portray the Portland branch! *Author*

'O2' class No. 189 waits to depart from Melcombe Regis with a Portland train at an unknown date between April 1924 and June 1932. Details to note are the three coal rails added to the bunker of these locomotives by the turn of the century to increase their coal capacity, and the guard who is wearing a conductor's cash bag, as part of his duties on the branch was to issue tickets to passengers boarding at unstaffed halts. No. 189 was constructed at Nine Elms works in October 1890 at a cost of £1,550, and was one of the few early withdrawals of the class, being cannibalised for spares in July 1933.   *Lens of Sutton*

In the days before works canteens a large number of men from Whitehead's factory travelled home for their dinner, albeit a rushed one. The train from Portland was strengthened with two extra coaches and the Southern goods engine assisted as pilot. 'O2' tanks Nos. 229 and 177 wait at Melcombe Regis to return the sustained workers to Wyke Regis Halt.   *Lens of Sutton*

A GWR '2021' class saddle tank hauls a mixed rake of four-wheel coaches across the wooden viaduct across the Backwater. This original structure of 1865 was replaced in 1909 by a fine five-span steel girder bridge.   *Author's Collection*

A view looking north-west of the five-span Backwater viaduct of 1909. The area in the foreground was later reclaimed for the construction of Melcombe Regis Gardens and Radipole Park Drive, whilst the area under the bridge to the left was reclaimed later becoming the Westham coach park.   *A. Hutchings Collection*

The absence of road traffic is noticeable in this 1930s photograph of Littlefield Crossing, viewed from Westham bridge. An 'O2' crosses with a Weymouth-bound train. Note the pre-war gates, with the wicket gate next to the crossing box. The subway can be seen to the right of the crossing, and the entrance to Westham coach park to the right. The original coach park was off Westwey Road to the left.   *Author's Collection*

The same view in September 2001. The Catholic church (*left*) and health centre (*right*) remain, as do the houses stretching away along Abbotsbury Road. The railway has gone, Westham bridge being closed to traffic and in use as a car park. Across the end of the bridge Westwey Road has been extended to form part of the ring road.   *Author*

Originally just a crossing keeper's cottage sufficed to protect the railway where it crossed the road to Westham, but as the suburb developed a raised ground frame (Littlefield Crossing) was erected in 1890 and a new crossing keeper's cottage constructed adjacent. Constructed with tile clad walls, it survived until road improvements obliterated the site in the 1980s. *W. Newman*

At Littlefield Crossing, crossing keeper Jack Newman watches as an 'O2' with a former LSWR corridor set heads towards Portland during the late 1940s. *W. Newman*

A view taken after October 1946 from the end of Westham Halt, looking through the crossing towards the viaduct and Melcombe Regis. To the left is the crossing keeper's cottage and on the right Littlefield Crossing ground frame. From the outside this gave the impression of being a full-blown signal box. *Lens of Sutton*

The same view taken in September 2001. In the foreground is the 'cycleway' to Ferrybridge. Behind is a new road layout leading to Weymouth Way and the new bridge across Radipole Lake. *Author*

Two views from Littlefield Crossing box during the 1950s - *above*, looking towards Westham bridge with Southern National Bristol K5G No. 871 (JUO 975) approaching with the 20A service to Westham. No. 871 was new to Weymouth depot and remained until withdrawn at the end of 1965, spending many years on the Westham services 20A/B/C. *Below* '57XX' pannier tank No. 9620 passes Westham Halt with a Weymouth-bound goods. *(Both) Author's Collection*

Littlefield Crossing viewed from Westham Road during the early 1960s. Note the advert for daily excursions from Weymouth to London 32s.! The crossing formed the boundary between Abbotsbury Road to the right, and Westham Road to the left. The two houses in the background with windows of the same style as the crossing box, although fronting onto Westham Road were 'Stavordale Villas' - Nos. 1 and 2 Stavordale Road.   *Author*

Silhouetted against the sky an 'O2' and a four-coach 'gate set' climb the Marsh embankment towards Rodwell with a Portland train. The new harbour wall of Westwey Road crosses the picture and the new gas works extension appears on the right.   *Author's Collection*

Photographed from the top of Rodwell tunnel between 1874 and 1880, this view clearly shows how little existed on the Westham side of the Backwater at that time. In the top centre the original viaduct can be seen curving across the Backwater, and above it is the large outline of the original Weymouth station goods shed 1857-1880. Behind the Railway Arch Tavern only part of Marsh Road has been constructed. The gas works is above the tree in the centre, whilst to the left open land awaits development. *Author's Collection*

A view from the top of Pye Hill before 1904 showing the Marsh embankment curving across the centre. A vast amount of development has taken place during the 25 years. Although the power station has not yet been constructed, all the open land around the Portland branch on the Westham side of the viaduct has been built upon. *Author's Collection*

An aerial view of the Marsh embankment taken during the 1920s. A six-coach Portland-bound train is crossing Newstead Road arch. The power station and original gas works occupy the centre of the picture. The land alongside the harbour has not yet been reclaimed for the construction of Westwey Road or the extension of the gas works that later filled the lower corner of the harbour. Today the east side of the harbour is now unrecognisable with recent developments.

Author's Collection

Looking through Rodwell tunnel with a train disappearing towards Weymouth before the 1907 alterations. With forethought the 58 yds-long tunnel was constructed for double track, although with the later alterations only a catch siding was laid in the left-hand side.
R. Carpenter Collection

Rodwell pre-1914. A GWR saddle tank and train await departure for Weymouth. Note the allotment on the embankment bottom left. Until the World War II the staff at Rodwell were renowned for their horticultural prowess.   *Author's Collection*

Above: A delightful view of Rodwell station taken after a snow-storm. Looking towards Portland from the top of the tunnel the improvements of 1907 are clearly shown, with the signal box and pagoda shelter on the new up platform connected by a footbridge, and the original station building and down platform on the left. Rodwell was one of the few stations of its size to have no road access, the footpath down the embankment on the extreme left being the only means of approach.

The late E. Latcham Collection

Right: Rodwell on 24th July, 1939. 'O2' No. 185 eases out of the up platform onto the single line with a Southern goods for Weymouth, behind the vans is a substantial amount of stone traffic in open wagons. The signalman has already 'pulled off' allowing the departure of the 4 pm Melcombe Regis to Portland hauled by 'O2' No. 177 with a train formed of three GWR coaches.

J.R.W. Kirkby

A pre-1907 view of a GWR saddle tank departing Rodwell with a Portland-bound train. The train has just reached the summit of the Weymouth-Portland section of the line having climbed 80 ft in just over 1 mile. The cutting through the Lansdown Estate required several blasting operations during its construction, the material removed helping to build the Marsh embankment. *Author's Collection*

The bridge crossing the footpath at the bottom of Rylands Lane, between Sandsfoot Castle and Wyke Regis Halt. This view, taken in the years following World War I, shows small vessels at anchor in the west side of Portland harbour behind Whitehead's pier which can be seen projecting out from the right. In the background is Portland, with the Merchants' Railway incline clearly visible above the centre of the bridge. The bridge itself was renewed with a concrete structure on 14th April, 1957. *Author's Collection*

Above: An Ivatt class '2' tank passes the remains of Wyke Regis Halt with a Portland-bound goods in February 1965. To the left is the concrete wartime road laid alongside the line towards Ferrybridge - an emergency measure in the event of the road bridge being put out of action prior to D-Day.
Author

Right: During the late 1950s it was decided to up-rate the main electric cable supply to Portland from several 11,000KV cables to one 33,000KV cable. The section across the causeway was laid alongside the railway, the cable being unreeled from drums loaded on railway wagons, hauled by a pannier tank.
S. Morris Collection

Pannier tank No. 3765 awaits recovery from the hole caused by severe flooding near the Mere Crossing on the night of 26th October, 1949. A Bath & Portland Stone Firms AEC Monarch lorry deposits one of the many loads of rubble required before the line was restored.

Author's Collection

Portland Beach Road flooded along the section between the Mere Crossing and Victoria Square, but only in exceptional circumstances did the railway cease to function. Note the abandoned cars and motorcycle alongside the road. Behind the dividing wall in the foreground stands the Portland 'down main home' and 'main to goods yard' signal and above the left-hand car 'Portland up advance starting ' and 'goods yard starting'. The oil tanks and the island form a backdrop to this bleak winter scene.

S. Morris Collection

Passengers travelling to Portland between 1865 and 1905 would have arrived at this imposing stone building facing Victoria Square. This was closed when the new passenger station situated on the curve towards Easton opened, but continued to serve as the goods depot until closure in 1965. The Portland branch goods traffic was sufficiently important for Portland to retain the post of station master until August 1962. *Author's Collection*

Construction of the new Portland station early in 1905, viewed from the mudflats known as 'The Mere'. The amount of infill required for its construction can be appreciated! Through the scaffolding on the left can be seen the name board 'Portland' and to its right part of the canopy of the waiting shelter forming the temporary station serving Easton trains between 1902 and the opening of the new station. *British Railways*

The exterior of the new Portland station shortly after opening, with several horse-drawn conveyances standing by. A liveried groom and other bystanders pose for the cameraman, capturing for posterity the Edwardian scene.   *Author's Collection*

The visit to Portland by His Majesty King Edward VIII on 12th November, 1936. Having spent the night aboard the Royal train in the flooded goods yard, His Majesty is seen after inspecting members of the British Legion assembled in the station approach, as he proceeds to his car for the journey to the dockyard. To his left is Commander Lord Louis Mountbatten, the King's personal *Aide-de-Camp*.   *Author's Collection*

Portland station staff photographed not long after the opening of the new station at Portland in 1905, their uniforms displaying the W & P badge worn on the hat. Seated in the front row is station master James Laver who stayed at Portland from March 1892 until June 1914. He had previously been station master at Shepton Mallet GWR for 15 years. Being a joint station his position at Portland required a great deal of discretion when dealing with matters that could affect both or either railway company.   *Lens of Sutton*

The new Portland station of 1905 viewed looking towards Easton, showing the sharp curve and the open timber construction of the platforms necessary to restrict the weight on reclaimed ground.   *The late J.H. Lucking Collection*

Signalman Bernard Lee and station master G.H. Jenvey stand by the temporary lever frame installed at Portland following the bombing of the signal box on Sunday 11th August, 1940. Behind is a hut erected to house the instruments and telephones. *Author's Collection*

Ivatt class '2' 2-6-2 No. 41293 shunts Portland yard on 6th February, 1965. To the right is Portland signal box, a structure of 'air raid precaution' design built following the destruction of the previous box on 11th August, 1940. The contract for the new structure was signed with Weymouth builders Messrs Theo Conway Ltd on 22nd March, 1941 at a price of £805. This would have been for the structure only, the GWR adding the fittings and lever frame. The new box was brought into use on 29th September, 1941. *Inset:* The Great Western Railway was usually very definite about the names of its signal boxes, always being apostles of the obvious and ending with the words 'signal box'; however, no doubt to save materials in war time 'Portland' was succinct! *(Both) C.L. Caddy*

An interior view showing the block shelf with the GWR type instruments and the 33-lever 4 inch vertical tappet lever frame. By the time the photograph was taken in 1963 many of the levers were out of use and painted white. *M.R. Thresh*

'O2' No. 201 stands in the down platform at Portland on 7th July, 1934, by which time the original wooden platforms had been rebuilt of solid construction. No. 201 was constructed at Nine Elms works in July 1891 at a cost of £1,660. She was transferred to the Isle of Wight in May 1947, renumbered W34 and named *Newport*. In August 1955 she became one of the first two of the Isle of Wight 'O2' class to be withdrawn, and was scrapped on the island.   *Lens of Sutton*

'O2' No. 220 stands at Portland station with a train consisting of GWR stock. No. 220 was constructed at Nine Elms works in January 1892. Transferred to the Isle of Wight in May 1930 as No. W18 *Ningwood* she was the only 'O2' returned to the mainland, being shipped back to Eastleigh for overhaul in early 1947 before returning to the island until finally withdrawn in December 1965.   *Lens of Sutton*

An aerial view of Underhill taken during the war, showing the Chesil, Castletown, and Fortuneswell areas. The Verne Citadel and its moat dominate the upper centre of the picture. Portland station is at the bottom centre with the line curving away through Castletown and past the Dockyard to the left. Bomb craters on the hill between the Dockyard and Verne show near misses to this vital establishment. 1. Portland station. 2. Portland goods depot. 3. Chesil Beach. 4. Fortuneswell. 5. Castletown pier. 6. Site of stone loading piers 1825-1897. 7. Merchants' Railway incline. 8. Merchants' Railway incline, brake drum. 9. Course of Merchants' Railway. 10. Royal Naval Hospital.   *Crown Copyright*

An aerial view of Portland station taken in May 1947, looking towards Chesil Beach. The railway curves across the picture towards the station at the top centre, with the road to Castletown crossing at an angle from the left, and Castletown sidings curving off just below where the road crosses the railway. The buildings to the bottom right are near the entrance to Castletown pier, and the pre-1897 stone loading piers were situated where the buildings are standing below Portland Castle. *HMS Osprey*

Bomb damage at the junction between the Easton line and the Dockyard sidings, photographed on 23rd August, 1940. Although the Dockyard sidings had been restored to use, the Easton line in the foreground had to wait until more important damage elsewhere had been attended to. The sandbagged building to the right was the former seaplane hanger of earlier days. See photograph page 32. *British Railways*

Construction work on the two bridges carrying the Easton line over the east end of the Dockyard, and the Admiralty incline running down from the Grove. Looking towards Easton across both bridges, the incline passing under the second and ascending to the right.

Author's Collection

Looking through the second bridge (known to railwaymen as 'Birdcage Bridge'). In the foreground are the rails and guide rollers of the Admiralty incline, and in the background the breakwater and Naval ships at anchor. *Author's Collection*

Looking towards Easton following the landslip near Grove Point on 27th November, 1907. The severity of the movement can clearly be seen and the platelayers are resigned to the fact that 'The best length prize' will not be theirs that year! *Author's Collection*

Looking towards Portland, after work has commenced on clearance. It was calculated that over 30,000 cubic yards of earth and rock had moved over a 300 yd length. The line remained closed until 23rd December. *Author's Collection*

A GWR saddle tank has brought wagonloads of ash to the site for infill. The large number of men shovelling out the material gives an indication how labour intensive permanent way work used to be.   *Author's Collection*

Looking down on the line at Grove Point shortly after the 1907 landslip. The reinstated section can be clearly seen with the train climbing towards Easton.   *Author's Collection*

The sheer rock face is clearly shown as an 'O2' climbs and turns away from the cliff face into the cutting at Red Bridge before the final climb around the bottom of Wakeham up into Easton station. *E.D.K. Coombe*

Not only were the skills of a good workman required, but also a good head for heights and nerves of steel were necessary, as clearly demonstrated in these views taken during the construction of Red Bridge.

Author's Collection

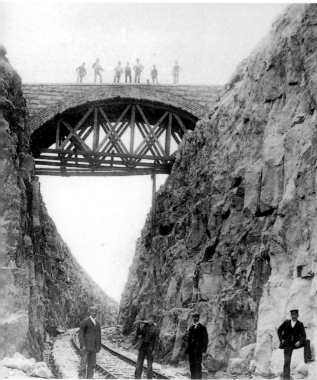

Left: Work in progress during the construction of Red Bridge.
Author's Collection

Below: Red Bridge viewed from Wakeham, looking towards the cliff. To say parts of the Easton line 'were not built but quarried' would be no understatement. Note the fence posts on the right are of the galvanised steel-variety popular at that period.
Author's Collection

Even these two views do not do justice to the steepness of the Easton line. Above, an unidentified 'O2' storms up the final cutting and around the curve towards Easton at 'Quarry Tip Siding', which climbs away to the right, whilst in the lower illustration in the foreground the line from Portland steeply descends and curves left towards Wakeham and Red Bridge. The siding climbing away in the background is 'Quarry Tip Siding'. To the left 'Bottomcombe Siding' and headshunt are shown.   *Author's Collection*

Easton station during the late summer of 1898. It was reported that by October the station roof was ready to receive its slates. In the foreground is the temporary track laid for the contractor's locomotive, around which the workforce are assembled for the benefit of the photographer.
Author's Collection

Easton, viewed from the Portland end, with the work of construction almost complete. A contractor's muck wagon stands in the platform road, whilst spare sleepers lie by the signal box.
Author's Collection

Above: Easton station, viewed looking towards Portland. Although the signal box had been constructed the signals had yet to arrive, and it was to be a further two years before passengers would be able to avail themselves of the station's facilities.
K. Lynham Collection

Right: The gutted booking office of Easton station following the fire of 28th November, 1903. It seems to have interested the local inhabitants, who are making a close inspection of the damage! *Author's Collection*

The construction of the bridge over the line in Reforne during 1899. The building behind on the right later became Fancy's Garage, where yet another part of the island's transport history took place with the operation of char-a-bancs and the Portland Express bus service.

Author's Collection

The bridge leading from Victoria Place over the railway into Sheepcroft Yard. In the foreground on the right is the single-lever ground frame operating the catch points which protected Easton station from run-away wagons from Sheepcroft Yard. This was provided after the spectacular run-away and smash of September 1903.

Author's Collection

Easton signal box photographed during the 1930s with roses around the door. The box and signalling equipment for the station were supplied by Evans O'Donnell of Chippenham, the lever frame consisting of 14 levers. Points Nos. 7, 10, and 14 were fitted with economic locks, a system that reduced the length of the frame by working both points and lock from the same lever.

Author's Collection

Easton station, following rebuilding after the fire of 1903, with - to the left - the engine shed added in 1905. In this typical Edwardian scene the lady holds a parasol to protect her from the sun. The railway official standing third from the left is Percival H. Brayley, station master 1905-1915.

Author's Collection

An unidentified 'O2' waits to depart from Easton. The locomotive still retains its original stove pipe chimney (several of the class retained them until the late 1920s). Although taken after the erection of the engine shed in 1905, Easton had an air of timelessness about it, but this photograph is considered to be pre-1920. *John L. Flann Collection*

Easton station, looking north during the 1920s with 'O2' No. 189 standing in the platform before departing with a Weymouth train.   *Author's Collection*

Photographed from the same position 70 years later, nothing except a very shallow cutting remains to indicate that a railway station once stood on the site. Ladymead Hall, residential accommodation for the elderly, now occupies the site, whilst either side the houses of Broomfield Terrace and Channel View Road are all that remain of the old scene.   *Author*

'O2' No. 177 waits to depart from Easton on 28th May, 1929. The painters are busy repainting the station, like others on the branch in GWR colours, a contrast to the Southern Railway locomotives and stock used for the regular service. No. 177 was something of a celebrity engine on the branch, having appeared by the late 1920s she remained until the end and hauled the last scheduled passenger train from Portland to Weymouth on 2nd March, 1952. *H.C. Casserley*

'O2' No. 217 stands at Easton during the early 1930s, the 'gate' arrangements being clearly visible on the leading coach. Note the coal bunker constructed of old sleepers and used to store the station and signal box coal supply, safe from those who might wish to appropriate it for their own use! No. 217 was shipped to the Isle of Wight in May 1936 as No. W16 *Ventnor*, where she remained until withdrawn from service in December 1966 at the end of Island steam operations, and broken up the following summer in Newport goods yard. *Lens of Sutton*

Looking down on Easton station from Reforne road bridge during the late 1930s. 'O2' No. 193 has just arrived with a train from Weymouth. To the right is the small engine shed and the houses of Station Road and Channel View Road. No. 193 was built in November 1890 and survived until April 1962, being one of the last four mainland members of the class to survive until that year.   *Lens of Sutton*

The signalman descends from the signal box at Easton as 'O2' No. 221 waits to depart in this 1930s view. Built in September 1892, this fine example of Victorian engineering gave 61 years of service before being withdrawn in August 1953.   *Lens of Sutton*

'O2' No. 213 photographed whilst running round its train at Easton during the late 1930s framed in the footbridge linking Bloomfield Terrace and Station Road. This plate-framed bridge had recently replaced the original latticework structure, although for reasons unknown the maker's plate from the original structure of 1899 had been transferred to the new bridge and is clearly shown! *Lens of Sutton*

'O2' No. 233 runs round its train at Easton station on 29th August, 1938. The end detail of 'Gate Set' No. 371 is clearly shown. No. 233 was the last Western Section engine to run with the 'E' prefix before its number, not becoming plain Southern Railway No. 233 until repainted in July 1935. Built in January 1895, she was withdrawn from service in February 1958. *J.R.W. Kirkby*

The Final Years

Between 1949 and the closure to regular passenger traffic in March 1952, the rolling stock changed in early 1951 from an assortment of GWR coaches to the use of the two articulated sets from the Isle of Sheppey branch. Set No. 513 was formed by coaches Nos. 3660 and 975 painted in green, and set No. 514 coaches Nos. 3561 and 976 in British Railways red livery. Although the later years and closure were not recorded to the same extent as the mass closures of the 'Beeching' era, those photographers who visited the branch have left us a good record of the events of the period.

'O2' No. 233 enters Melcombe Regis station with a train of GWR stock ready to form a service to Portland on 4th June, 1949. In the foreground tank-traps remain as a reminder of the importance of the Portland branch during the war years. Away to the left are the new Jubilee Sidings of the 1930s on land reclaimed from Radipole lake. On the land in the left foreground stood the 'Centenary Club' of the Staff Association between 1957 and 2001. *John H. Meredith*

'O2' No. 30179 with a train consisting of GWR stock runs into Portland station with a train from Easton on 14th June, 1949. The large oil tank on the right is part of the gravity system used to transfer oil between the Mere tank farm and the Dockyard. The building on the extreme left is the Naval Officers Club, later to become a major part of the helicopter base. *R.A. Lumber*

'O2' class No. 30177 waits to depart from Easton with a Weymouth train during 1950. The first of the class, built in December 1889, this particular locomotive cost £1,615 to build and gave good value for money, remaining in service until October 1959. As No. 177 this locomotive had made its appearance on the Portland branch by the mid-1920s, an association she was to maintain until withdrawal of passenger services in 1952. *Lens of Sutton*

'O2' class No. 30223 heads across the causeway near 'Black Hut' with a Weymouth train on 14th July, 1951, the former Isle of Sheppey articulated set being one of the only two sets of articulated stock on the former Southern Railway. *R.H. Tunstall*

Climbing the Marsh embankment past Newstead Road, 'O2' class No. 30231 heads a Portland train towards Rodwell. Owing to the almost non-existent luggage space in the articulated sets the PMV vehicle next to the engine was required when these sets were used.   *R. H. Tunstall*

An evocative picture capturing the atmosphere of a winter's day as 'O2' class No. 30197 hurries away from Portland across the causeway with a Weymouth train consisting of one of the former Isle of Sheppey articulated sets, shortly before closure in 1952.   *Dorset Daily Echo*

'O2' class No. 30230 departs from Easton with a Weymouth-bound goods shortly before closure to passenger traffic. In the foreground is the headshunt from Easton goods yard, the line curving away to the right being originally known as Webber & Pangbourne's siding.

The late J.H. Lucking Collection

The exterior of Easton station on 16th February, 1952. When built the officials of the GWR and LSWR reported 'The Easton Company have built a station at Easton without first consulting the joint Companies. It is a matter of regret that plans were not submitted as suggestions would have been made to improve the arrangements'.   *John H. Meredith*

Time for reflection, as railway staff and a passenger are engaged in conversation at Easton station in February 1952, a few days before closure. The engine, 'O2' class No. 30179, was built in March 1890 and gave 69 years' service before being withdrawn in December 1959.
Author's Collection

'O2' No. 30197 crosses the entrance to the outer section of Weymouth goods yard on 16th February, 1952 hauling former Isle of Sheppey articulated set No. 514.   *John H. Meredith*

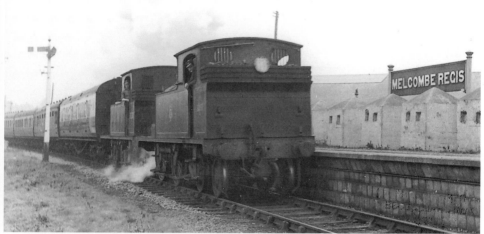

'O2' tanks Nos. 30197 and 30230 draw into Melcombe Regis with the stock to work the 1.15 pm to Easton on Saturday 1st March, 1952. As there was no Sunday service over the Portland-Easton section, many people travelled on the Saturday, this being their last chance before closure. Main line stock was pressed into service as the articulated sets would have been completely inadequate for the crowds. *D. Cullum*

The fireman of No. 30197 looks back to ensure the train is 'inside clear' in the loop at Rodwell whilst working one of the strengthened service trains to Easton on Saturday 1st March, 1952. The inside locomotive is No. 30179. Although the signalling and signal box at Rodwell were of GWR origin, a SR rail-built signal (shown pulled off) had already replaced the original GWR wooden down starter. *W. Newman*

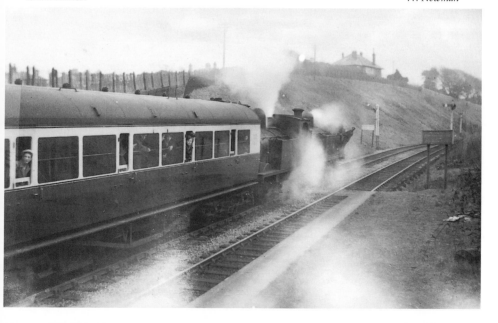

'O2s' Nos. 30197 and 30179 climb up past Grove Point with an Easton-bound train on the last day of regular passenger services to Easton on Saturday 1st March, 1952.   *Lens of Sutton*

'O2s' Nos. 30179 and 30197 run out of the cutting under Red Bridge onto the cliff top section descending towards Grove Point with the 3.17 pm Easton-Weymouth service on Saturday 1st March, 1952.   *D. Cullum*

'Specials' and Goods Traffic

Following the withdrawal of passenger services the station buildings at Portland and the waiting huts at Westham, Rodwell, Sandsfoot Castle, Wyke Regis Halts were removed, together with the signal boxes at Rodwell and Easton and the signalling was simplified over the next two years.

Although enthusiast railtours were in their infancy, the Portland branch featured in a number during that period. Also classed as 'special traffic' would be the Royal Train, Naval specials, and engineers trains which often ran at short notice and therefore were not photographed.

Pannier tanks Nos. 7784 and 9642 head towards Littlefield Crossing with a Naval special for Portland in July 1955. Between the locomotives and the crossing keeper's cottage, in the background can be seen the rides of the funfair that occupied a corner of the Westham Coach park site. *W. Newman*

Nos. 9642 and 7784 depart from Portland station with a Naval special during July 1955. Today No. 9642 is preserved at the Dean Forest Railway. In the background housing development had begun on Verne Common, and behind the train the gasometer of Portland gas works is visible. *W. Newman*

Pannier tank No. 4624 passes under Wakeham Road bridge on the final climb to Easton whilst working the Railway Travel & Correspondence Society 'Wessex Wyvern' special that toured various Dorset branch lines on Sunday 8th July, 1956. In recent years this section out to the cliff has been used as an internal road by lorries to reach quarry workings.   *R.H. Tunstall*

'M7' class 0-4-4T No. 30107 with push-pull set No. 378 stands in the remains of Portland station on Sunday 7th June, 1957 whilst working the Railway Enthusiasts Club special which toured various Dorset branch lines. The main station buildings had been demolished in April 1954, but the platforms remained intact - as did the footbridge. At that time there was a dispute concerning the right of way over it and the footpath from Castletown Road bridge.

J. Spencer Gilks

'M7' class No. 30107 with push-pull set No. 738 stands at Easton station on 7th June, 1957 with the Railway Enthusiasts Club special. It was an historic event, being the last visit of a passenger train formed of LSWR (stock and the first time for many years) and the final time that LSWR stock actually worked in push-pull mode over the branch.   *J.W.T. House/C.L. Caddy Collection*

During the 1950s Melcombe Regis was often used during busy periods as an extra platform for Weymouth station. An unidentified light Pacific complete with a train of Bulleid stock in red and cream stands at the platform just short of the viaduct. On one occasion - unfortunately not photographed - a GWR 'Castle' class actually pulled forward and crossed the viaduct stopping adjacent to Westham coach park! Such use of Melcombe Regis involved the Portland signalman being on duty to release the key token at Weymouth Junction signal box enabling a train to enter the section.

The late J.D. Blackburn

Pannier tanks Nos. 3737 and 4624 head across the causeway from Portland on 29th April, 1959 hauling the nine-coach Royal Train conveying Her Majesty The Queen and HRH Prince Charles, following their visit to HMS *Eagle* at Portland. The first Royal visitor to use the Portland Railway had been Prince Alfred on 29th November, 1865. The 1959 visit was to be the last Royal Train to travel over the branch and the last passenger train to leave the Dockyard.   *The late J.H. Lucking*

Pannier tank No. 3737 descending under Red Bridge with the return working from Easton of the Railway Correspondence & Travel Society's special over the branch on 14th August, 1960. On the return journey the train was stopped at the Mere Crossing and searched by the police who were looking for two escaped Borstal boys, but it continued to Weymouth with its number of passenger undiminished!   *I. Shorter/C.L. Caddy Collection*

'57XX' class 0-6-0PT No. 7780 in charge of a permanent way train stands on the causeway just south of Ferrybridge on 2nd September, 1962. A careful inspection of the locomotive will reveal a bell fitted below the tank between the cab and the tool box, operated by a length of cord pulled by the fireman from the footplate. This was used when the locomotive was employed on the Weymouth Harbour Tramway.   *C.L. Caddy*

Pannier tanks Nos. 3633 and 4689 propel a weed killing train through Rodwell on 7th June, 1963. The upper photograph clearly shows the chemical, which is stored in the tank wagons, being sprayed onto the ballast from the pump van. *(Both) M.R. Thresh*

On a wet foggy Sunday 25th August, 1963 0-6-0PT No. 4689 enters Easton station with the Southern Counties Touring Society special. The seven-coach train included a buffet car, this being the only known occasion when one of these vehicles ran over the Easton section of the line. Pannier tank No. 7782 pushing at the rear would become the leading engine for the return journey. *Author*

Pannier tank No. 7782 stands at Easton at the head of the Southern Counties Touring Society 'Southern Counties Enterprise' on a dull wet 25th August, 1963. *John H. Meredith*

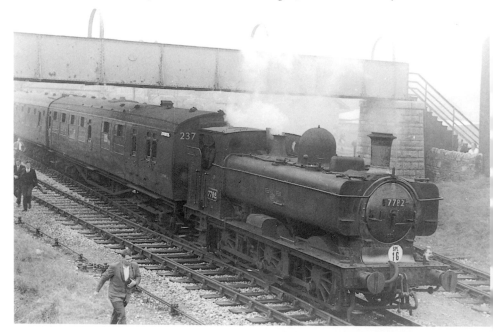

Demolition of the buildings at Rodwell took place during 1954. Already the pagoda hut on the up platform has been dismantled, and the down side hut is under demolition. These were followed by the footbridge and signal box, leaving the two platforms that remain to the present day. *The late J.D. Blackburn*

'57XX' class pannier tank No. 9620 draws a line of empty wagons up the incline from Easton into Quarry Tip Siding for loading on 11th June, 1958. *The late J.H. Lucking*

'57XX' class pannier tank No. 9620 shunts wagons at Quarry Tip Siding on 11th June, 1958.
The late J.H. Lucking

Sheepcroft Yard on 29th October, 1960, with 0-6-0PT No. 4624 standing in the loading dock loop whilst shunting. From the left are, Reg Pavey, fireman Vic Powell, driver Eddie Miller and guard Jack Townsend. *Author's Collection*

Pannier tank No. 7780 shunts Portland yard on 6th January, 1962. This engine was built in 1930 by Armstrong-Whitworth of Newcastle-on-Tyne, one of 200 pannier tanks built by outside firms as part of a Government scheme to alleviate the depression. No. 7780 was withdrawn in 1963 following a collision with another engine in Weymouth engine shed!

C.L. Caddy

No. 3633 shunting Portland yard on 4th June, 1963,. The second guard's van was to accommodate a party from Weymouth Grammar School who were privileged to travel over this 'goods only' line. No. 3633 was only allocated to Weymouth for a short period; she had been constructed at Swindon in July 1939, and was withdrawn from service in October 1963.

M.R. Thresh

Above: Pannier tank No. 3737 climbs the Marsh embankment towards Rodwell tunnel on 1st June, 1963 with a Portland freight. Much of this traffic was bound for the Channel Islands, being taken to Portland goods shed for checking and documentation before proceeding to Weymouth Quay for loading onto the Channel Island steamer.

C.L. Caddy

Right: 'Stuck'! Severe frost caused Ivatt class '2' 2-6-2 tank No. 41305 to slip to a standstill on the Marsh embankment on the morning of 10th November, 1964. Assistance had to be given from Weymouth by sister engine No. 41374 to push the train over the summit at Rodwell.

The late J.H. Lucking

Ivatt class '2' 2-6-2T No. 41261 crosses the bridge leading to the main part of Westham coach park in March 1965 with a Weymouth-bound goods. In the foreground is a Bedford SB of Swanage Coaches and a Bedford VAL of Cosy Coaches of Parkstone.   *C.L. Caddy*

Ivatt class '2' No. 41261 crosses Chickerell Road bridge with a Portland-bound goods on 25th February, 1965. The keystone of the bridge, carved with the Prince of Wales feathers, was ceremoniously placed in position by Mr Maunders, the Weymouth & Portland Company Chairman, on 10th March, 1863, the Prince's wedding day. The Railway Arch Hotel on the right replaced the previous Railway Arch Tavern shown on page 47.   *Author*

Ivatt class '2' 2-6-2 tank No. 41324 passes over Newstead Road arch on 21st January, 1965 with a Weymouth-bound freight. Situated at the centre of an 'S' bend its narrow confines were a traffic hazard, and prior to the construction of the new Westham Bridge in 1921, traffic of any weight had to use this route to gain access to Westham. During the reconstruction of the Town Bridge in 1929-30 the GWR bus service to Wyke Hotel was diverted via Westham Bridge and Newstead Road.   *C.L. Caddy*

Demolition of the arch in February 1987 to allow road improvements in connection with the new supermarket built on the site of Weymouth football ground.   *Author*

Ivatt class '2' 2-6-2 tank No. 41298 climbs the Marsh embankment away from Westham Halt on 18th February, 1965 with a freight for Portland. *Author*

Ivatt class '2' 2-6-2 tank No. 41293 pounds through the remains of Rodwell station with a Portland-bound freight in February 1965. The loop on the left, although still in position, had been 'clipped out of use' since March 1954 when Rodwell signal box was closed. *Author*

Ivatt class '2' 2-6-2 tank No. 41261 runs down past the remains of Wyke Regis Halt with a Portland goods in February 1965. The footbridge to the cliff footpath is in the background, and the sidings into Whitehead's factory to the left.   *Author*

The same view in September 2001. Only the trackbed in the foreground remains, the embankment on the left has overgrown both the platform of the halt and the trackbed, the footpath being on the wartime concrete road that ran alongside the railway.   *Author*

Ivatt class '2' 2-6-2 tank No. 41293 climbs away from Portland with a short goods for the Dockyard on 6th February, 1965. Behind it lays the remains of Portland station and part of the Royal Naval air station stands on the right. *C.L. Caddy*

The same location photographed in September 2001. All traces of the line have disappeared, an oil pipeline being laid along part of the formation. The nearby buildings and the Naval air station have also passed into history. *Author*

Ivatt class '2' 2-6-2 tank No. 41293 climbs past Castletown Junction on 6th February, 1965 with a short freight for the dockyard. The building in the background is the former Naval hospital, and the siding in the foreground leads to Castletown Yard, which in pre-war days formed an exchange point with the wagons of the Merchants' Railway. Their last use was in 1957, as a storage place for some of the large fleet of 'Palvans' built for the Channel Islands traffic but subsequently found unsuitable.

C.L. Caddy

Final Closure

The final closure of the branch was marked by the running of three special passenger trains on Saturday 27th March, 1965 organised by a small local society, The South & West Railway Society. The trains were made up of six main line coaches with an Ivatt class '2' tank at each end. However owing to delays in arranging the new facilities at Weymouth goods shed, goods traffic continued until 9th April, 1965 when the final train used the branch.

Viewed from Grove Point on Saturday 27th March, 1965 one of the last day specials coasts down from Easton towards the Dockyard. Class '2' 2-6-2 tank No. 41284 the leading engine blows off steam, whilst sister engine No. 41324 trails at the rear.   *Dorset Evening Echo*

Ivatt class '2' 2-6-2 tank No. 41284 waits to leave from Easton with the last-ever passenger train to depart on Saturday 27th March, 1965. *C.L. Caddy*

The final passenger train headed by Ivatt '2' 2-6-2 tank No. 41284 commences the downhill run into the cutting from Easton station on Saturday 27th March, 1965. *C.L. Caddy*

Ivatt class '2' tank No. 41284 passes Portland signal box heading for Weymouth with one of the last passenger specials run on 27th March, 1965. *Author's Collection*

The very last passenger train from Easton enters the remains of Portland station on Saturday 27th March, 1965. 'Portland Station Signal Box' (1905-1935) was situated just off the platform to the right of the locomotive. *Author*

On 27th March, 1965 one of the last special passenger trains between Weymouth and Easton heads back towards Weymouth across the causeway. Nearest the camera Ivatt class '2' 2-6-2 No. 41324 propels the train whilst in the distance sister engine No. 41284 is the leading engine.

C.L. Caddy

Just after 9.30 am on Friday 9th April, 1965 the very last train to travel over the Portland branch departed from Melcombe Regis, headed by Ivatt class '2' 2-6-2 No. 41284. It consisted of one wagon (for collecting tools and other equipment) and a brake van, and cleared remaining wagons from the branch on the return journey. The final train of nine wagons and brake van arrived at Weymouth Junction at lunch time, thus closing what was once Dorset's busiest branch line six months short of its centenary. The Railway Staff Association 'Centenary Club' on the left opened in 1957, closed in October 2001 and was demolished, making way for a fast food outlet.

D.M. Habgood

In February 1966 demolition commenced on Melcombe Regis station buildings to make way for the construction of a garage to maintain British Railways lorries. The actual platform face remained for another 24 years. *C.L. Caddy*

Melcombe Regis station following the construction of the Road Motor Department workshop on the site of the station building. To the left the roof of the Channel Islands shipping 'provedore' store built on the station approach road can be seen, whilst part of the trackbed has been removed to make way for a go-cart track. Beyond, the Backwater viaduct awaits demolition. *Author*

Track removal taking place at Easton during the early part of 1967. The entire Easton & Church Hope Railway was removed to its junction with the Admiralty line.   *Author*

Contractors remove 'Birdcage bridge', which crossed the road between the Dockyard and HMS *Osprey*. This had originally been the course of the Admiralty incline for bringing stone down from the Grove for the construction of the breakwater.   *Author's Collection*

The entrance to Portland Dockyard viewed in the summer of 1967. The line towards Easton has been removed and a landslip has already covered its course and spilled onto the Dockyard entrance to the left. *Author*

A general view of Portland yard in the summer of 1967 following the removal of all track except the line to the Dockyard curving away to the left. This was retained for a further two years while a decision was awaited as to whether it would be required in future. *Author*

The interior of the original Portland station, which had been used as a goods shed since 1905, photographed in April 1967 following the removal of the track. The original timberwork of the roof is clearly shown as is the lean-to roof and wall on the right which had been added early in 1896 to protect passengers from the elements blowing in off Chesil Beach.   *Author*

The removal of the level crossing gates and demolition of Littlefield Crossing ground frame taking place on 30th April, 1969. A view through the remains of the gates towards the Backwater viaduct. The tile-hung crossing keeper's cottage is on the left.   *Author*

Work commenced on 13th September, 1970 on removal of the track between Portland station and Weymouth. Commencing at Portland the rails were cut into short sections, then removed by mechanical shovel ready for collection by road transport. By early 1971 recovery had reached Westham Halt, where workmen are shown cutting the rails into sections for transportation.
Author

Contractors commence demolition of Ferrybridge during 1971. With the fast flowing current of the Fleet it was not the easiest of tasks, a small fishing vessel being used to assist with the work.
Author

The demolition of the Backwater viaduct became a somewhat protracted affair, commencing in November 1974 when the first span at the Melcombe Regis end was lifted out in two sections. Work proceeded well lifting out the second span side sections, the mobile crane working with ease from the car park where the sections were cut up and removed by road. *Author*

Work degenerated into farce when removing the sections over Radipole Lake. The intention of dropping them into the water and dragging them ashore failed to go to plan, resulting in work having to be suspended during the summer of 1975, whilst people hiring rowing boats on the lake had to navigate around buoys to avoid becoming shipwrecked! *Author*

The removal of the piers was achieved with a mixture of explosives and a good pull with a wire
from a winch. One of the centre piers starts to fall in late 1975. *W. Macey*

A former GWR and LSWR boundary marker set into a plaque on the wall of the guardroom at the entrance to the Royal Naval heliport which occupied the site of the former Portland station. Today, like the railway, the Navy has also departed, the guardroom has been demolished and the site is awaiting future development. *W. Macey*

Clearing the remains of Melcombe Regis station in June 2000 prior to the building of 'Swannery Court', a block of luxury flats. The demolition of the platform removed the last vestiges of the Portland branch from the area. *Author*

Preservation

Of the many locomotives that regularly worked the Portland branch, three are now in preservation. Although the branch is now just a memory, a visit to many of the heritage railways around the country will clearly demonstrate how our railways operated in the age of steam.

'57XX' class pannier tank No. 9642, constructed at Swindon works in April 1946, was during the early 1950s allocated to Weymouth Shed and worked the Portland branch freight duty. Withdrawn from service in November 1964 and sold to R. & S. Hayes, scrap dealers of Bridgend, she was found to be in good condition and she was used to shunt the scrap yard thus avoiding the fate of others until purchased for preservation in February 1968. She moved around several preservation sites before arriving at the Swansea Vale Railway in April 1989. At the time of writing No. 9642 resides at the Dean Forest Railway, Lydney, where she was photographed working a demonstration train *above* at Norchard Road and *below* on the unopened section at Parkend on 26th September, 1998.   *(Both) R.C. Clammer*

Right: Ivatt class '2' No. 41298 in store at Quainton Road in October 1986. The last Ivatt to receive a general overhaul at Eastleigh works in 1964, she worked the Portland branch up to closure in 1965. Her final claim to fame was working the last steam train over the Weymouth Harbour Tramway on 3rd April, 1966. After restoration it is proposed to transfer No. 41298 to the Isle of Wight Steam Railway, following in the footsteps of other former Portland locomotives. *Author*

Below: To the enthusiast the 'O2' class will always be associated with the Portland branch. From their introduction they worked the LSWR passenger traffic and from World War I onwards all passenger traffic until withdrawn in 1952. No. 209 was constructed at Nine Elms works in December 1891 at an estimated cost of £1,625, transferred to the Isle of Wight in April 1925 where, renumbered 24 and named *Calbourne*, she continued to haul Island trains until the end of steam in 1966. She was then retained for engineering work during electrification of the Island line until March 1967 when she was sold to the Wight Locomotive Society for £900. Today restored with her original small bunker, she works on the Isle of Wight Steam Railway. It is believed No. 209 was allocated to Dorchester during the early 1900s in which case she would have worked Portland trains. Today she is the sole survivor of a class that served the Isle of Wight and the Isle of Portland with distinction. *J.E.R. Jackson*

Weymouth and Portland Motor Bus History

The first motor bus service in Weymouth commenced in June 1905 when the Great Western Railway ran a service between Wyke Hotel and Radipole Spa Hotel, via the King's Statue. It was introduced to safeguard the railway from the possibility of various electric tramway schemes which Weymouth Council were discussing at that period, ranging from a short route between Radipole and Wyke Hotel and a through service between Upwey and Portland in conjunction with Portland UDC. By the time the various schemes were last discussed in 1910 the Portland branch had been up-graded and halts added on the main line at Radipole and Upwey, thus reducing the chance of success of any tramway.

The GWR buses remained, apart from a short spell between September 1909 and July 1912 when they ceased to operate owing to a disagreement with Weymouth Council. Following World War I various char-a-banc companies started up at both Weymouth and Portland, but although they were able to win a limited amount of excursion trade they had little effect on the Portland branch or the GWR buses.

The arrival of Road Motors Ltd at Weymouth in October 1921 and the commencement of a service between Upwey and Portland Victoria Square was the first challenge to branch line traffic. In May 1924 Smith - a local Portland operator - commenced a bus service between Victoria Square and Portland Bill, providing the first service to 'Tophill'. The National Omnibus & Transport Company (NOTC), who between 1922-1924 operated a seasonal service into Weymouth from Bridport, acquired both the Weymouth Motor Company and Road Motors Ltd early in 1925 - providing them with a good foothold in the area - and in February 1927 took over the Portland local service operated by Smith. Acquiring several other routes in the Weymouth area from local char-a-banc operators this company and the GWR held between them a monopoly on stage carriage services. In 1929 with the split-up of NOTC, their name was changed to 'Southern National', the railway companies acquiring a large shareholding in the new company and others in the Tilling group.

The GWR Weymouth service (except for short-lived extensions to Upwey, Chickerell and Preston following World War I) never expanded and was the last GWR bus service to survive, being taken over by Southern National in January 1934.

However, by that time both the Southern National and the railways had a new competitor in the form of 'Portland Express'. Three Portland char-a-banc proprietors, Messrs Fancy, Hoare, & Tolman set this up and commenced a limited stop service in May 1932 between Portland Bill and Weymouth, King's Statue. It proved very successful, the new venture posing a threat to both the Southern National and the railway companies, who in July 1936 purchased the undertaking, the service being absorbed into the Southern National operation.

By the late 1930s all the private operators in Weymouth had either ceased trading or had been taken over by Southern National except one, Dean of Chickerell, who operated a summer tours programme from Westham coach park, whilst on Portland the surviving operators had limited licences which restricted their operations.

The war years severely curtailed any further expansion of services as both bus and railway companies struggled under mounting difficulties and the

Above: GWR Milnes Daimler No. 58, LC 1172, stands at Wyke Hotel before departing for Weymouth and Radipole during 1905. This early vehicle was powered by a four-cylinder 18/20 hp petrol engine driving a four-speed gearbox giving road speeds of 3, 5½, 7 and 12 miles per hour. The lubrication system was primitive, and although there were three separate brake systems, stopping the vehicle was not an exact science!

D.F. Hollings Collection

Right: GWR Milnes Daimler No. 58 stands outside Saltash railway station in 1920, a clear demonstration of the quality of the Milnes Daimler chassis. It had operated from Saltash during World War I, for a time running on coal gas. This vehicle had been one of the first two GWR buses to operate from Weymouth and gave the company 15 years service - a record as good, if not better, than many later vehicles.

John Cummings Collection

problems of the austerity years that followed. Hoare, trading as 'Bluebird Coaches' had continued with his coachwork following the sale of the Portland Express syndicate, and in 1940 had moved from Portland to Chickerell, taking over the business of Messrs Dean. Following the war he commenced to operate tours from Westham coach park and in the ensuing years built up a flourishing business.

On Portland the Smith family re-entered the coach business in 1947, operating private hire and a few tours, but a licence for a stage carriage service to Weymouth was refused in 1952. By the early 1950s only 'Pump' Saunders remained of the pre-war Portland independent operators carrying out some private hire work and running a restricted stage carriage service between Castletown and Weymouth. He sold the business to Smith in February 1962, which gave the latter a stage carriage licence, although he did not actively pursue the business.

In Weymouth the Bere Regis & District Motor Services opened a garage at Radipole in 1953, operating mainly private hire and works contract services. There were picking-up restrictions on their tours' licences, which handicapped that side of the business.

Southern National continued to expand, the convenience of the bus service being the cause of a drastic fall in passengers using the Portland branch. Its closure to passenger traffic in March 1952 gave Southern National the monopoly of passenger trade along the Portland route.

GWR Milnes Daimler No. 66, AF 192, approaches the Town Bridge, Weymouth, from the bottom of St Thomas Street. The shop on the right, Strong Williams (a well known local ironmonger), was demolished in 1937 for an intended road widening scheme. To the left, a horse-drawn hotel bus waits outside the Crown Hotel.   *Maureen Attwooll Collection*

Mr Percy Boyle, Traffic and Marine Agent for the GWR at Weymouth Quay, driver 'Taffy' Williams and conductor George Priest stand by GWR Maudslay No. 1210, YR 6218, at the King's Statue. Note the bracket-mounted oil side light between Mr Boyle and driver Williams; the latter is wearing his light summer coat whilst George Priest is still in full winter suit, the cash bag and bell punch ticket machine showing up clearly.   *Author's Collection*

A delightful early 1930s seaside view of Weymouth Esplanade. Just caught by the camera is a rear view of a GWR Maudslay approaching the King's Statue. It clearly shows the roof luggage rack and ladder. To the right of centre one of the few remaining horse-drawn wagonettes waits to take passengers to Upwey Wishing Well.   *Author's Collection*

The inscription on the back of this postcard reads 'Driver Peters at Longhill on Portland trip'. The vehicle is EL 874 a 1912 vintage 30 hp Lacre char-a-banc owned by George Bugler of Rodwell Mews, Weymouth who was one of the few pre-World War I operators. This vehicle had been new to Mark Briant of Bournemouth, and was converted into a lorry during 1916.
Author's Collection

The first motor bus service between Weymouth and Portland commenced in October 1921 when Road Motors of Luton started a regular service between Radipole Spa Hotel and Portland Victoria Square. Certain journeys were extended to Upwey Royal Oak. Road Motors No. 4, BM 5375, a 26-seat Palladium, stands at Upwey Royal Oak before departure to Portland. In the background a train climbs towards Upwey Wishing Well Halt and Bincombe tunnel.

Author's Collection

Weymouth Motor Company Ltd Daimler 'CK' type Daimler char-a-bancs FX 5962, FX 5961, and FX 5923 complete with passengers pose for the camera during an excursion. These vehicles later joined the National fleet upon take-over and gave further service until the early 1930s.

Author's Collection

FX 5042, a Daimler 'CK', was the first char-a-banc purchased by the Weymouth Motor Company Ltd in November 1919. With the take-over of the company by the NOTC it acquired fleet No. 2230. With Charlie Bateman at the wheel it is about to depart with an excursion from Weymouth Esplanade. *The late E. Latcham Collection*

By July 1926 a Dodson OT30/26R body had been fitted. The vehicle had also been transferred to the eastern part of the NOTC empire, where it was photographed at the head of a line-up about to depart on an outing. Placed into the Eastern National fleet in December 1929, it later passed to Dawson, a dealer of Clapham, London. *The late E. Latcham Collection*

One of the earliest photographs of a National bus at Weymouth. AEC 'YC' type No. 2173, NO 9540, stands in Great George Street about to depart with a service to Bridport and West Bay. New to the National fleet in 1923, 2173 was originally fitted with a char-a-banc body which was quickly exchanged for the 30-seat bus body shown. Standing alongside is driver Sidney Hurford who came to Weymouth as a young man with the National buses and remained until retirement, becoming the company's longest serving driver. *The late E. Latcham Collection*

AEC 'YC' type No. 2065, AD 7310, with a Dodson OT30/26RO body stands outside the Hotel Burdon (now the Prince Regent) on Weymouth Esplanade, with conductor Dominy alongside. Note the long white coats worn by staff at that period. Originally 2065, of 1920 vintage, was fitted with a OT22/22RO body. This vehicle later moved to Eastern National territory and was withdrawn in 1932 from Bedford depot. *The late E. Latcham Collection*

A lesson on where not to put your hands when having a photograph taken! Driver Percy Applin (*on the right*) and conductor Arthur Gardner centre stand by PR 2459, a GMC 14-seat bus of Smith and Hoare's fleet. The fleet name 'Portland Bus Service' is showing on the side. It operated a service between Victoria Square and Tophill. This vehicle passed to NOTC in 1927 as No. 3290 and was disposed of to Messrs Morris of London in August 1929.   *Author's Collection*

Portland char-a-banc drivers and friends pose for the cameraman at Castletown pier, with 'Molo' Hansford driving, Don Pike standing by the engine, Leslie Tolman sitting behind the driver. three of the other four are known to be Pepperal, Wykie, and Fred Brown. The details and ownership of this left-hand drive Ford model 'T' are obscure. As with many char-a-banc photographs the photographer never included the entire vehicle or showed the number plates.
      C. Tolman Collection

JT 4140, photographed near the end of its life, this Bedford WTB with a Duple C26R body was new to Fancy of Portland in January 1936 and was quickly absorbed into the Southern National fleet with the take-over of 'Portland Express'. Requisitioned by the War Department from Weymouth garage on 13th July, 1940, it was purchased from a surplus Government sale in 1944 by Russell of Wormington, Gloucestershire, and re-registered as FAD 827, remaining in service with the local operator until 1951 when acquired by contractors Messrs Costelloe & Kemple of Cheltenham for a further year's service. *(Both) J. Russell Collection*

The coach that never returned, Bluebird Dennis Lct 2, JT 1528, was requisitioned by the War Department in June 1940, and later placed with Mid Wales Motorways. The shielded headlights and white tipped wings suggest the photograph was taken before the end of hostilities, the vehicle still carrying the Bluebird livery and fleet No. 2. *Omnibus Society*

Above: AEC Regal TK 7892 of Victory Motors of Weymouth turns at the Borstal Institution, Portland during an island tour. Passing into the amalgamated Victory/Greyhound fleet and later sold to Southern National becoming fleet No. 3582, she was fitted with a new Duple C32F coach body in 1940 and transferred to North Devon, and is seen there, *below,* at Bideford Quay on 18th August, 1946. No. 3582 was eventually sold for scrap in 1954.   *(Both) Omnibus Society*

Above: A view of the King's Statue, Weymouth after May 1935 when the one-way system was introduced. Buses stand awaiting passengers, but the coaches have already departed on tours. In later years getting to the middle of the road to catch a bus became a hazardous business! *Author's Collection*

Right: Western National No. 3440, YD 3862, a Dennis Lance new in May 1932 to Dunns of Taunton, was acquired by Western National when Dunn's services were taken over. It had a Duple L28/24R body with the unusual feature of a straight staircase on the nearside. Purchased by the Royal Navy on 1st July, 1940, it was later re-registered as RN 6812 and used as mobile training unit for Asdic Equipment. She later turned over on Portland Beach Road and was disposed of for scrap in December 1943. The driver, Len Ralf (*on the left*), later spent 19 years as a driver for Southern National at Weymouth. *Author's Collection*

One of the only two known photographs of a Southern National six-wheeler taken on Portland. One of the redoubtable Leyland TS7D, 44-seat Beadle-bodied six-wheelers Nos. 1000-1005, they carried the bulk of the Tophill traffic between 1937 and 1953. Viewed here from the Britannia public house in Fortuneswell during a snowstorm in the final years of its life, she is followed by two of the Bristol LS saloons that replaced them on Tophill services.

R.E. Diment Collection

Following the closure of the Portland branch in March 1952 pupils of Weymouth Grammar School had to travel by bus. Southern National Bristol LS5G/ECW B45F No. 1683, LTA 980, waits to depart from the top end of Westwey Road where originally the school buses picked up and dropped off. No. 1683, new in 1953, was withdrawn in 1970, then passed to Valliant Cronshaw of Hounslow for further service. *The late E. Latcham Collection*

Six of Weymouth's coach fleet line up for a publicity photograph at Portland Bill in 1954. from left, Nos. 1374, OTT 83; 1341, LTA 997; 1378, OTT 87; 1344, MOD 971; 1379, OTT 88 and 1375, OTT 84. These Bristol LS6G ECW-bodied vehicles gave the company excellent service. In 1969 No. 1379 was still operating long distance Express services and tours during her final year.

Author's Collection

Whilst working a service to Littlemoor (33B) on 13th January 1962 No. 1842, LTA 952, came into contact with the grab of a crane clearing shingle from Preston Beach Road. Fortunately there were no passengers sitting 'up front' at the time! The photograph clearly shows the recessed wheels of the 7 ft 6 in. chassis fitted to an 8 ft wide body. This 1951 Bristol KS5G was withdrawn in 1969.

Dorset Daily Echo

WEYMOUTH AND PORTLAND MOTOR BUS HISTORY

Standing in the doorway of the Dorchester Road garage of Bere Regis & District Motor Services is Leyland PS1/1 MTJ 444, fitted with a rare King and Taylor C33F body. New to Silver Grey of Morecambe in 1950 it was acquired by Bere Regis & District in 1955, and finally withdrawn in 1968. Standing on the left is depot manager John Woodsford, and on the right fitter Paul Hyde.

John Woodsford Collection

During the first month of double-deck operation to Tophill, FLF No. 2048, 428 PTA, swings around Priory Corner heading for the Grove on 25th January, 1969. New in 1964 this H28/32R ECW-bodied vehicle was withdrawn during 1978 and passed to a Yorkshire dealer.

C.L. Caddy

Two pre-war view of Westham coach park, photographed from the Backwater railway bridge. The top view looking towards the coach park entrance and Westham bridge. A dozen coaches of different types can be seen. At the top right a coach of 'Dean' of Chickerell waits on its stand to operate a tour. The bottom view, looking north, again shows a fine selection of vehicles of the period. Before the fire of August 1930 Spivey's garage was situated where the coaches stand on the bottom left. The wooden hut in the background belonged to a scout group.
(Both) G. Pritchard Collection

The Day Tripper

Being a seaside resort Weymouth was visited by many char-a-bancs and coaches; as vehicles improved so the distance they travelled to reach the resort increased. In the early days the few parked in Gloucester Mews, no doubt obtaining petrol and perhaps mechanical attention at either A'Court's Royal Garage or Spivey's Weymouth Motor Company garage.

By the late 1920s parking space had become a problem, one plan being to fill in part of Weymouth Harbour between Westham Bridge and the weir to form a coach park. In the event, space was provided at the north end of Westwey Road, (later the site of Weymouth's first Public Library). Within a few years this was unable to cope, and as land on the west side of Radipole Lake to the north of the Backwater viaduct was gradually being reclaimed this provided the ideal site. There was the low brick arch under the Portland branch railway, but as coaches were single-deck this did not cause a problem, and by the late 1930s the site was in use.

Following the war more infilling extended the site, and the 1950s saw it used to full capacity, a good Summer Sunday bringing in excess of 200 coaches to the resort. The record stands at 364! Although coaches were smaller 29- and often 35- and 37-seaters, being conservative and allowing each coach 34 passengers, that accounts for 12,376 day trippers who crossed Westham Bridge and walked up Westham Road to the Esplanade and the sands on that one day. They also returned at tea time, the shops in the few hundred yards of Westham Road were a gold mine, fish & chip shops, cake shops, fruit shops, a cafe, and others all ready to serve the needs of the many!

Whereas the coaches usually arrived between 10.30 am and 1 pm, nearly everybody departed at 6 pm, causing congestion as coach after coach crawled across Westham Bridge to the King's Statue and up the Esplanade. In 1971 the coach park moved to Lodmoor on the eastern edge of the town, well away from the sands and the town centre, a 'park & ride' service of buses being provided to the King's Statue. Already declining in numbers, the day-tripper trade quickly fell away and within a few years the park & ride was withdrawn. The loss of the coaches at Westham indirectly caused the closure of both the fairground and miniature railway, these having relied upon the day-tripper trade.

The scenes of the 1950s are gone forever. It was a procession of every chassis and body combination imaginable, ranging from pre-war to the latest model, of many liveries and owners from the humble village operator to large coach companies and the Tilling and BET groups. An inspection of the boot doors, with the owner's name usually displayed in sign writing was a gazetteer of Wilts, Somerset, Dorset, and much further afield. Many of the fleets are now just memories: Wems, Rimes, Charlies Cars, Wessex, Chard & District, Darch & Willcox, Roman City, just to name a few.

There were events that stayed in the memory; about six Swindon Corporation CVD6 Daimler single-deck, Park Royal-bodied centre-entrance buses parked up on a private hire. Six or more Wilts & Dorset double-decks on an excursion, these having to park on the Westham Bridge side of the railway arch, as did the Harrisons of Clapton, ex-Glasgow Corporation, double-deck GE 2427 - a 1929 Leyland TD1 with Cowison body in a dark blue livery which worked a daily summer service from Crewkerne. Later taken over by Chard & District, the Leyland was replaced by a 1945 Daimler CW6A, HWB 491, new in 1945 to the Sheffield Corporation B fleet. Looking smart in the Chard & District fawn and red livery, its journeys to Weymouth ended in July 1955 when it was damaged at Upwey when flash floods struck the area.

Changes at Portland Bill followed the same pattern as at Weymouth, in the early days it was purely local char-a-bancs. A typical summer afternoon during the 1950s would see the local tour operators of Weymouth, Dorset and the surrounding counties well represented. However, times have changed, and today many coaches seen at the Bill are on extended tours to the area having travelled considerable distances.

Photographed at Westham coach park is GE 2747, a 1929 Leyland TD1 with Cowieson H28/31R bodywork. New to Glasgow Corporation as No. 92, it had passed to Seager of Sherborne, Dorset by August 1945, and was sold to W.G. Harrison of Royal Blue Coaches of Clapton, Crewkerne, Somerset in September 1948. It worked its daily summer service between Crewkerne and Weymouth during the summer of 1949; with the take-over of Harrison's by Chard & District Motor Services in March 1950 this vintage vehicle was disposed of in the May.   *B. Thompson Collection*

The Bus Services 1969-2001

Southern National Bristol LS5G No. 1701, OTT 55, on display at the 1979 Weymouth Bus Rally having just been restored to the traditional Southern National Tilling green and cream livery. Built in 1954, 1701 became the last operational LS within the NBC, having spent the majority of her working life at Weymouth, and today is in the care of the Science Museum.   *Author*

Whereas Volume Three of *The Isle of Portland Railways* specifically ended the story in 1969, subsequent developments require it to be updated. The 1968 Transport Act allowed the creation of the National Bus Company (NBC), which took over the bus interests of the Transport Holding Company (THC) from 1st January, 1969. Southern National, a former part of the Tilling Group which had been absorbed into the THC, automatically became a unit of the newly formed NBC. It was the beginning of a new era of bus operation. In the following years sweeping changes were to take place.

Breaking what had been a taboo from the beginning, on 5th January, 1969 double-deckers commenced to operate to Portland Tophill, the service also being extended from the King's Statue through to Radipole Spa Hotel. At that time Southern National operated all local stage carriage services, a selection of tours and a portion of private hire work. Bluebird, the sole survivor of the pre-war independent operators carried out contract, private hire work and had a seasonal tours operation from Westham coach park, whilst on Portland, Smith carried out contract and private hire work. Bere Regis & District, having closed its Radipole Garage in 1967, still undertook a small amount of private work in the town from its Dorchester depot.

However, another operator was about to appear on the scene. Barry Newsam, who had previously operated a taxi service, acquired an 11-seat mini-bus in June 1966 and, having obtained an operator's licence, commenced private hire work. By January 1968 he had obtained his first full size coach, a Ford/Plaxton C41F, which was followed by several midi-coaches. Upon enlarging the business, the vehicles were kept in a yard at the rear of a shop in Buxton Road. Further expansion moved the business to the Granby Industrial estate, trading under the fleet name of 'Barry's Coaches'.

The Westham Bridge bus only lane in operation. *Top*, a view looking across the bridge towards Littlefield Crossing and Abbotsbury Road. *Centre*, a bus pulls into the entrance to the bus-only lane and the driver presses the post-mounted button. *Bottom*, traffic has stopped from Abbotsbury Road and Westwey Road (*left*) whilst the Westham-bound bus proceeds across the bridge.

Radipole garage in February 1968, with the cast concrete word 'National' on display. Usually this was covered by a painted 'Southern National' sign. The 'National' dated back to 1929 in which year the original Road Motors garage was enlarged. On the forecourt stand Bristol MW6G ECW C39F coaches Nos. 1416, EDV 554D; 1419, EDV 549D and 1414, EDV 544D, in the blue and cream livery applied to new coaches after 1963.   *C.L. Caddy*

One of the last major events of 1969 was the complete renumbering of Southern National Weymouth and Portland area routes into the 400 series on the 8th June. In January 1970 the company ceased to exist as a separate operation, being absorbed into the larger Western National, but apart from a change of fleet name little else altered. In 1972 the fleet started to lose its familiar Tilling green livery in favour of the new NBC leaf green, with an enlarged fleet name in white block capitals with the new 'double N' symbol next to it, and the replacement of the traditional black uniforms worn by bus crews with grey and a cap modelled on that of an American policeman.

Throughout the 1970s small changes were taking place, mainly adjustments to routes and timetables often caused by the decline of bus usage. On 1st June, 1970 a new one-way traffic system was introduced in Weymouth with the novel feature of a 'bus only' lane against the flow of traffic across Westham Bridge. This was controlled by a button on a post which was pressed by the driver, this changing the lights at the Westwey Road junction to allow the bus free passage across the bridge towards Westham.

During 1981 the monopoly Western National had enjoyed on local fare stage services since 1936 was to end. Smith's of Portland although still only operating private hire, contracts and tours, had outgrown its Easton Square premises and in January 1977 moved into the former Southern National garage in Victoria Square, later acquiring the former Aitcheson's garage and the house next door. Despite obtaining Saunders' licence in 1962, and renewing it every three years as required, no services were operated - although the fare table was updated. This particular licence, the last remaining of those

Despite all prophets of doom anticipating a serious accident with double-deckers climbing to the top of Portland, the only accident of any note was on 25th July, 1973 when the driver lost control of FLF No.1982. It came to rest six feet from the edge of a quarry in Wide Street after leaving the road, demolishing a telephone pole, and ploughing through a compound of scrap cars. Had it proceeded further it could well have been the most serious bus accident ever to occur in the area. *Dorset Evening Echo*

granted to the Portland independents, was badly worded and caused problems when issued in 1931, the full story of which is explained in Volume Three.

Following events at a Traffic Commissioner's hearing at which Barry's Coaches were granted a tours' licence, Smith commenced a service from Portland Bill to the Jubilee Clock, Weymouth, on 1st May, 1981. However, with just two services a day departing Weymouth at 9.40 am and 12.40 pm and Portland Bill at 11.38 am and 2.38 pm it had little effect on Western National, although the fares were lower. By March 1982 Smith's had increased the number of journeys and by charging a lower fare a price war developed as Western National reduced its fares below the level of Smith's. The King's Statue-Victoria Square fare was reduced from 65p to 25p, King's Statue-Easton from 80p to 40p, and Portland Bill from 95p to 55p.

No doubt owing to the ambiguous wording of the licence the matter was disputed by Western National, resulting in a Traffic Commissioner's inquiry at Weymouth Guildhall on 7th October, 1982. Over 100 supporters arrived in two coaches, a 1,345-signature petition and over 200 letters of support having been handed in. Indeed, such interest and support was rare at a local hearing and not known since the pre-war Portland Express dispute. Smith was granted a renewal of the firm's licence to run 10 return journeys Monday-Friday, six on Saturday and three on Sunday.

Allegedly proposed expansion by Barry's Coaches and the threat of competition on lucrative Weymouth routes led to an agreement whereby the Dorchester Town Service, which Southern National had acquired from the 'Dorchester Motor Services' in 1935, was handed over to Barry's Coaches, together with the Dorchester-Wool and the Wool-Bovington Camp services on 26th July, 1982. Under the fleet name 'Interbus' Barry's had expanded dramatically, commenced other rural services and obtained a tours & excursions' licence.

To celebrate the 50th anniversary of the last GWR omnibus service, two Weymouth-based VRTs, Nos. 608 and 1158, carried commemorative plates at the end of 1983.   *Author*

By the early 1980s the Government wanted to divest itself of the bus industry, so it then became NBC policy to break the companies up into smaller units that would be attractive for privatisation. Thus Western National was split on 1st January, 1984, and Southern National was reborn with main depots at Weymouth, Yeovil and Taunton where a head office was established.

During the summer of 1984 Nigel Charlton, trading as 'Weybus', obtained an operator's licence and acquired a minibus, later commencing to operate on several routes in the Weymouth area. October 1986 saw him operating a County Council-subsidised service to Osmington Mills, and a Weymouth-Chickerell service in the evenings. By the summer of 1987 he had expanded into Littlemoor Estate one of Southern National's most lucrative routes! As the Weybus operation continued to expand, the events of the pre-war Portland Express dispute paled into insignificance.

Southern National introduced its first minibus services into Weymouth on Monday 14th July, 1986, when many local services were taken over by a fleet of Ford Transit/Robin Hood B16F vehicles in a yellow, blue and orange livery and branded as 'Weymouth Shuttle', operating on a 'Hail & Ride' system.

The 1985 Transport Act came into force on 26th October, 1986, from which date bus services were freed from the Road Service Licensing system, which had originated under the Road Traffic Act of 1930, and were therefore now open to competition. Under de-regulation those services that operators considered unprofitable to operate were in many cases not registered as 'commercial' with the Traffic Commissioners and were withdrawn, but such services, if considered socially necessary by local authorities, could be subsidised by seeking tenders from operators for their provision. More importantly, no longer was an operator protected once he had obtained a licence for a route. Previously any other operator had to prove to the Traffic Commissioners that there was a genuine requirement for extra services, and if granted, strict safeguards covering timetables and fares were applied to protect all parties. These were swept aside under the 1985 Act, and it was open to all comers providing they had an operator's licence and registered the route with the authorities. Fares to be charged and the timetable was the operator's choice or weapon, depending on one's viewpoint.

The once popular destination of Upwey Wishing Well, which until the 1980s had had a 40 minute service, had dwindled to but a few buses a day in the light of declining patronage, both this and the Upwey Royal Oak services being diverted at Littlemoor Corner to serve the expanding Littlemoor estate, thus providing a direct service from the estate via Dorchester Road.

Seeing an opportunity Messrs Pearce, Darch & Willcox of Cattistock commenced a service on 19th July, 1987 from Weymouth Pavilion and the King's Statue to Upwey Wishing Well, running four journeys during the afternoons on Monday-Friday, and hourly 11 am-5 pm Sundays employing a 1937 Bedford WTB and HOD 76, a 1949 Bedford OB. Despite advertising the idea of a vintage coach trip to Upwey it was not over successful and was withdrawn. Fortunately, both vehicles are now preserved.

Following deregulation Southern National re-entered Dorchester with a minibus service in April 1987 in competition with Interbus, but there was insufficient traffic for two operators and Barry's withdrew from Dorchester that October and concentrated on its private hire, contract and coaching operations at Weymouth. In January 1989 Bere Regis & District commenced its own Dorchester town service using full size vehicles.

Photographed at Weymouth Pavilion at the inauguration of the Upwey Wishing Well service on 18th July, 1987, is vintage Bedford WTB JT 8077 with a C25F Duple body. New to Sheasby, South Dorset Coaches, of Corfe Castle in October 1937, in whose service it remained for 30 years until sold to Cutler Bros of Clevedon (the late Adge Cutler of Wurzels fame), it passed to a Lydney preservationist until acquired by Pearce, Darch & Willcox in August 1985. Later the vehicle was sold to Isle of Wight owners and preservation.   *B. Thirlwall*

In September 1987 the fierce competition between Southern National, Smiths, and Weybus spilled over into threats of violence between bus crews, producing adverse comment in the local press. Later that same month Southern National made front-page news when many services had to be cancelled at short notice. A company spokesman told the *Dorset Evening Echo*, 'We are being hit by a chronic staff shortage. We just can't get qualified green and shuttle bus drivers, so when drivers are sick we are unable to replace them'. At the same time, engineering staff, inspectors, and drivers were being made redundant in preparation for privatisation!

The sale of the constituent companies of the NBC had commenced in July 1986, Southern National, the 69th to be sold, being purchased by its management on 29th March, 1988. They also acquired North Devon Ltd (Red Bus), a holding company, Cawlett Ltd, being formed. However, this event had not been without a little drama. In October 1987 the NBC had decided to reopen bidding for the purchase of six companies, including North Devon and Southern National. The NBC wished to reconsider the sales in light of its duties under the 1985 Transport Act, after becoming concerned about possible links between potential purchasers, Drawlane Ltd and Allied Bus Services Ltd. Drawlane Ltd was seeking a judicial review of the NBC decision which was rejected in the High Court, the judge finding the NBC had acted properly in pursuance of the Act.

During this period Smith's service had expanded considerably, the company becoming 'Smiths of Portland Ltd' in February 1983. The service level was increased in June 1984 and again in March 1986, on the latter occasion part of the service being diverted from Wakeham to run via Courtlands with some journeys operating via the Kimberlin Club on the Naval housing estate, and the Weymouth terminal was altered from the Jubilee Clock to St John's Church. However, at the same time Sunday services ceased, never to return. In April 1988 the service was increased to half-hourly and the Weymouth terminus cut back to the King's Statue, whilst on Portland some journeys were diverted via Park Estate and others via Sweethill Estate.

In February 1989 the Smith family decided to leave the industry, the property and business being purchased by David Milverton of Portland Plant & Commercial Services who used the yard of the former Aitcheson's garage to maintain his fleet of vehicles, whilst he continued the Smith's business managed by Rodney Smith until selling out to the Cawlett Group in July 1989. From October 1990 the service was revised to run in co-operation with Southern National, the Southwell-Portland Bill section being withdrawn from the winter timetable and the deviations via Park Estate, the Kimberlin Club and Sweethill were also withdrawn. The Tophill section of the route became Easton to Southwell via Courtlands. During this period Southern National managed the business on a consultancy basis and maintenance of vehicles was carried out at Edward Street under contract until full garage facilities could be provided at Victoria Square.

Early in 1994 several changes took place in the Cawlett Group. Firstly Smiths of Portland returned to private ownership being acquired by K.J.R. Rimmer - a Plymouth businessman - whilst on 17th March the main part of Bere Regis & District Motor Services (based at Dorchester) was acquired, although the licences were not transferred until 6th May. Re-organised as West Dorset Coaches and

Departing from Portland Bill on 30th May, 1995 is Leyland Olympian No. 1814, A686 KDV, the last vehicle built by 'Bristol' at their Brislington factory in September 1983. New to Devon General, it was acquired by Southern National in 1990 and sold to the Isle of Man six years later. It is now preserved by The West County Historic Omnibus and Transport Trust.   *J.D. Ward*

Leyland Olympian No. 1814, A686 KDV, is seen descending towards Priory Corner during May 1995.   *J.D. Ward*

trading as 'Dorchester Coachways', the old two-tone brown livery was replaced by white with an orange roof and grey skirt. The acquisition of this old established company was to prove fortuitous for the group in the light of future events.

At the end of October 1994 Weybus, which was operating between the King's Statue and Littlemoor estate, charged a fare of 70p. In retaliation Southern National - whose fare was 88p - repainted three Ford Transits in blue livery and commenced to operate route J at 70p. This was followed by Weybus starting up an hourly service on 5th December from the King's Statue to Wyke Regis, Park Mead Road, with intermediate journeys from Park Mead to Westham Cross Roads via Lanehouse Hill. Further expansions were made in March 1995 by opening a service to Downclose Estate, Weybus now covering four of Southern National's principal routes.

Although Smith's had gone back into private ownership in the summer of 1995 it and Southern National introduced co-ordinated fares and joint inter-availability of all tickets and passes. As the advertising stated, 'To offer you the best Weymouth & Portland bus service possible'.

On 30th October, 1995 Weybus made its greatest incursion into Southern National territory by commencing a Weymouth-Portland service every 15 minutes between 7 am and 7 pm, and on 6th November opened a Weymouth-Dorchester service, which also served the new Dorchester Hospital. On the same date Smith's, in retaliation for Weybus starting a Portland operation, commenced a 30 minute service between the King's Statue and Littlemoor at a flat fare of 30p. This resulted in a situation where the buses of three operators vied for trade from one estate, and the sight of all three operators queuing at stops became a common sight all over Weymouth and Portland. Not surprisingly the fares agreement was rescinded from 4th December. Minor timetable adjustments took place during March, and on 22nd April the Littlemoor service was extended from the King's Statue through Westham Estate to Hereford Road, again in competition with both Southern National and Weybus. At one stage the Smith's fare was 10p to anywhere in Westham!

Relationships between Southern National and Weybus had reached an all time low by early 1996, resulting in both operators being brought before the Traffic Commissioners that March, principally over the operation of their Weymouth-Portland services. At the inquiry both complained about the other's methods, Southern National stating that Weybus had failed to operate in accordance with its registrations, and Weybus that Southern National had behaved in a predatory manner.

Weybus claimed that Southern National had deliberately interfered with its operations by swamping routes run by Weybus to make them unviable. Its vehicles had been boxed in at bus stops and were unable to move. Southern National had also poached its drivers and intimidated others, thus leaving Weybus short of staff and unable to run a full service.

Southern National claimed that the Weybus service time of 48 minutes over the same route that took it 66 minutes was inadequate and they were unable to comply with their registration particulars. In practice Weybus placed vehicles ahead of Southern National services in an attempt to deny passengers the opportunity of using a Southern National service. Southern National placed

Waiting for the Town Bridge to close is Southern National Mercedes-Benz, Carlyle B29F No. 701, H906 WYB, standing in the 'buses only' part of St Thomas Street on 3rd July, 1998. Behind it is a Smith's minibus and two Southern National Ford Transits. This section of road was later closed to buses, services being rerouted via Lower St Albans Street.   *J.D. Ward*

Two of Weymouth's original 1986 Ford Transits, Robin Hood B16F minibuses Nos. 360, C922 GYD and 374, C936 GYD, proceeding along Custom House Quay on 9th October, 1999. At that time to allow the Hereford Road service to operate via the Town Bridge it was routed via the town centre back streets. Note the trackwork of the Weymouth Harbour Tramway in the foreground.   *J.D. Ward*

vehicles at Victoria Square and Derwent Road (Wyke Regis) in what it claimed was a defence ploy, not an offensive measure against Weybus. It was further found that both operators had improperly run their Park Mead Road services.

The conclusion was that the Commissioner, Air Vice Marshall Ronald Ashford, banned Southern National from operating service No. 1 Weymouth-Portland and service F Weymouth-Park Mead Road, and from registering any further services in the Weymouth area or increasing the frequency of buses on service X10 Portland-Weymouth-Dorchester until the beginning of April 1997, whilst Weybus was banned from registering any further local services in the Weymouth area for six months.

The former Southern National services were registered by West Dorset Coaches who, although another subsidiary of the Cawlett Group, traded as a separate entity with its own operator's licence. Adopting the 'Dorset Transit' fleet name, it legally circumvented the Traffic Commissioners' rulings and took over the Weymouth-Portland service on Saturday 1st June, 1996, and the Park Mead Road service from Tuesday 4th. The vehicles were operated from and garaged at the Southern National garage, Edward Street, although at the beginning of June only nine vehicles had been allocated to the service and several Southern National vehicles were to be seen 'on hire'- an event that frequently had to be repeated during the busy summer period. Ironically, whilst all these changes were taking place Southern National was operating legally to Portland Bill during the summer months with its No. 501 service, this not being affected by the Commissioners' ruling!

Smith's curtailed the King's Statue-Littlemoor section of the Hereford Road-Littlemoor route after 14th September, 1996, releasing vehicles for the Portland routes, and from 14th December the Hereford Road service was completely withdrawn. On 29th September, 1997 an hourly service between the King's Statue and Easton and the Grove was introduced.

Another twist in the Smith's story came in January 1998 when it was announced that the Cawlett Group, through West Dorset Coaches, had purchased Smiths of Portland for the second time in seven years. Both existing routes were replaced in May with a new half-hourly Littlemoor--Chalbury Corner-King's Statue-Easton-Grove service. The X1 Portland-London service of Dorchester Coachways and the once-weekly 123 Portland-Bournemouth service were transferred from Dorchester to Portland and re-registered by Smith's.

The bus war came to an abrupt end in July 1998 when Traffic Commissioner Christopher Heaps, following an appeal, withdrew the operator's licence from Weybus as the company was no longer of good repute. On Thursday 30th July receivers were called in and Weybus ceased trading. It was the end of a small company which was once referred to in *Transit* as 'The South Coast Stickleback, the Tiddler that won't go away'. However it had survived over 11 years, and at closure was quoted as carrying 10,000 passengers a week in the Weymouth, Portland, and Dorchester area.

Within weeks former Weybus driver Tony Douglass was granted an operator's licence and the Commissioner accepted that Weybus founder Nigel Charlton was of satisfactory repute to act as transport manager of the new Wessex Bus Company. Five former Weybus vehicles were acquired and a stage carriage service between Weymouth and Abbotsbury, together with school bus contracts, commenced.

Apart from many column inches in the local press, the bus war gave, for a time, the 60,000 inhabitants of Weymouth and Portland a most prolific service at the lowest fares for many years. But the public are fickle in their loyalties, and when there's a choice the frequency of service and (more importantly) the fare charged are the yardsticks by which a service is judged.

The Cawlett Group itself was acquired by First Bus on 8th April, 1999, the irony being that despite the dismantling of the NBC, privatisation and deregulation, Southern National again found itself, as in years past, part of a large combine.

As with most large concerns image is all-important. Southern National became 'First Southern National' and Smith's Coaches ceased trading as a separate company on 4th September, 1999. The Littlemoor-Chalbury Lodge-King's Statue section was replaced by diverting Southern National's No. 31 and the King's Statue-Grove section became Dorset Transit No. 11. The fleet of four coaches and 13 mini-buses was absorbed into First Southern National, and Portland garage ceased to be an operational depot. Smith's Managing Director Stephen Bosley, who had since March 1991 been responsible for and personally involved in the day to day operation of the depot, became manager of West Dorset Coaches.

On 1st November, 1999 the mini-buses on the Weymouth-Portland service were replaced by eight Volvo B6 Wright-bodied B36F single-decks, and at the same time the service was altered to commence and terminate in Commercial Road at the rear of the new shopping centre. Although several other local services also use the Commercial Road facility, there is no direct connection with other principal services, which still operate from the King's Statue, which is quarter of a mile across the town.

Centralisation and reorganisation took place on 22nd April, 2001, when both Dorset Transit and Dorchester Coachways ceased as separate identities, both being incorporated into First Southern National, West Dorset Coaches depot at Dorchester closed, all operations being based at Edward Street garage, Weymouth. Dorchester remained as a store for delicenced vehicles, Smith's garage at Portland also being used for storage until vacated at the end of June, the premises now being shared between a car repair business and a small local coach operator 'Wheeltrim Coaches'. Next-door, the yard of the former Aitcheson's garage had become the operating base of Wessex Bus.

On April 22nd the Weymouth and Portland services were subjected to a major reorganisation, the local services being revised as 'The Weymouth Metro' with schematic Underground-style route leaflets with colour branded routes, these also being exhibited on the buses with a coloured band and route details. August 28th saw a new zonal fare scheme being introduced, and day tickets made available for 3, 4, or 5 zones, which were cheaper than a return ticket for the same distance. There was widespread criticism of the fare increases from many quarters, although it was argued that fares had only risen to the level they were before the bus war!

The 'First Bus' image was taken further from November 2001. Although Southern National still continues as the operating company the fleet name was changed from 'First Southern National' to just 'First', thus after 71 years Southern National's association with Weymouth and Portland had ended.

The Bus Fleets 1970-2001

Although one-man operated vehicles had been used on many country routes since 1959, their first use on town and Portland services took place on Sundays and in the evenings during the winter of 1972. The following summer the first two VRT double-deck one-man operated vehicles (OMB) arrived and were used on the Edward Street-Portland Bill service. Surprisingly, the main Portland routes were the first to go fully OMB the following year, other town services remaining crew operated!

In December 1975 Weymouth had an allocation of 64 vehicles including 7 VRT, 16 FLF, 9 LD, 10 LH, 10 LS/MW, 4 RE, and 2 of the new Leyland Nationals. Two years later there were 13 VRT and 9 LN - although 21 FLF crew double-decks remained - but this was changed to 16 VRT and 18 LN by December 1979 with 13 FLF mainly employed on schools and works journeys. The summer of 1980 was the last for crew operation, and in November only FLF No. 2080 (in Sealink livery) remained for the Railway Station-Weymouth Quay contract, 21 VRT and 21 LN providing most services.

Following the demise of the open top summer service in the early 1960s, it was not until the late 1970s that an open-top vehicle again appeared in the area when one of the older Devon General Leyland Atlanteans (927) was transferred to operate the seasonal Weymouth-Abbotsbury-West Bay-Bridport service. The following year a newer vehicle (934) was used, and for the 1983 season a second vehicle (942) was added and a livery of cream and green adopted and names applied with local connections. A third vehicle (555) was added in 1985, followed by 559 in 1987. The Bridport route had been abandoned and a series of services between Osmington Mills and Portland Bill, and the Pavilion Theatre to Bowleaze Cove route, were introduced. The cream and green livery was also changed, 559 had received a bright yellow livery with blue and red relief, this later being applied to all open-tops. In 1999 Nos. 555 and 559 were named *Henry Frier* and *Brenda Isaacs* respectively, after two retiring members of staff. During 1997-8 two open-tops were hired from Vintage Yellow Bus, of Bournemouth, and a fifth open-top was acquired in September 1998. Owing to there being an operational requirement for only three open-tops during the 2001 season, the two convertibles (934 and 942) were not used for open-top operation.

Apart from the open-tops several other vehicles have carried a branded livery. In April 1981 No. 3400, a DP C34F LH coach, appeared in dark green and white to advertise and operate the new X35 limited stop service between Weymouth and Bournemouth, branded as 'Southern Coastlink'. With the service later extended to Portland, in January 1983, VRT No. 1087 received a variation of the livery which was predominantly dark green. In May 1986 VRT No. 602 took over, painted in a revised livery of lighter green and white.

The other examples of special liveries were FLF No. 2080, receiving a white 'Sealink' livery in March 1979, and later LN No. 2823 which also towed a former London Airport bus luggage trailer. In 1985 several coaches received a local coach livery of white, brown, and yellow, which was said at the time to emulate the railway Pullmans!

The beginning of Weymouth's open-top bus revival, Devon General Leyland Atlantean No. 927, 927 GTA, stands alongside No. 934, VDV 134S, at Edward Street depot on 25th May, 1978, at which time the Devon General livery was retained.   *Author*

Following a competition held with local school children, newly converted VRT No. 555 was named *Sir Christopher Wren* by the Mayor of Weymouth & Portland, Councillor Peter Harvey, at Portland Tophill Junior School in June 1986.   *Author*

Western/Southern National Weymouth-based open-top vehicles

No.	Reg No.	Chassis	No.	Body	Type	No.	Built	Acq.	Notes
927	927 GTA	Leyland Atn	602644	MCCW	CO44/31F		5/61		1
934	VDV 134S	Bristol VRT	VRTSL3/1023	ECW	CO43/31F	22427	1977		2 8
942	VDV 142S	Bristol VRT	VRTSL3/1175	ECW	CO43/31F	22435	1978	1983	3 8
555	ATA 555L	Bristol VRT	VRTSL2 518	ECW	CO42/32F	20074	1973		4
559	ATA 559L	Bristol VRT	VRTSL2 536	ECW	CO43/31F	20078	1973		5
	ERV 249D	Leyland Atn	L44729	MCW	O44/33F		1966		6
	ERV 252D	Leyland Atn	L43855	MCW	O44/33F		1966		6
	CRU 180C	Daimler FL	60938	Weymann	O43/31F				8
560	MBZ 7140	Bristol VRT	VRT SL3 442	ECW	HO43/31F		1976	9/98	7

Notes
1. Renamed *Admiral Hardy* by Western National retained Devon General red/white livery.
2. Renamed *Thomas Hardy* by Western National in 1983.
3. Renamed *Lawrence of Arabia* by Western National in 1983.
4. Converted to open-top 1985 named *Sir Christopher Wren*, renamed *Henry Frier* 1999.
5. Converted to open-top 1987 named *William Barnes*, renamed *Brenda Isaacs* 1999.
6. On hire from Vintage Yellow Bus Bournemouth summer 1997.
7. Painted in overall advertising livery for 'Waterside Holiday Park', Bowleaze.
8. Convertible to open-top.
9. On hire from Vintage Yellow Bus, Bournemouth, summer 1998.

Previous Owners
927 New to Devon General as No. DL 927 named *Sir Martin Frobisher*.
934 New to Devon General as No. 934 named *Golden Hind*.
942 New to Devon General as No. 942 named *Hermes*.
560 Ex-Stephenson, Rochford. New to East Midland as No. 151, 8/76. To Stagecoach, Scotland.
ERV 249D New to Portsmouth Corporation as No. 249. Owned by Vintage Yellow Bus, Bournemouth.
ERV 252D New to Portsmouth Corporation as No. 252. Owned by Vintage Yellow Bus, Bournemouth.
CRU 180C New to Bournemouth Corporation as No. 180.

At privatisation Southern National retained the NBC green and white livery (without, of course, the NBC symbols), but after experimenting with several liveries apple green and cream was selected for the main fleet, with the mini-buses continuing to have yellow as their base colour. These liveries remained until the takeover by First Bus, when their livery of magenta, pink and grey was introduced, nicknamed 'Barbie Livery' because of its similarity to the packaging of Barbie Dolls. This was applied to new vehicles of high specification, older vehicles retaining a modified version of their local company livery. The first Weymouth bus to receive this was Mercedes No. 703, H908 WYB, in July 1999. Towards the end of 2000 this started to be replaced by a revised 'Barbie' livery unofficially known as 'Barbie 2'.

The first Leyland Olympian double-decks appeared at Weymouth during 1987, two having arrived from West Yorkshire PTE, a further batch being obtained from Devon General in 1990. The Olympians were the first vehicles at Weymouth with fully automatic gearboxes. Amongst the 1990 acquisitions was No. 1814, A686 KDV, the last vehicle completed at the Bristol factory in September 1983 before closure, thus ending 75 years of chassis production. Fortunately this ECW-bodied H45/30F example was sold in 1996, along with other Olympians, to Isle of Man Transport. As No. 57, MAN 57N she was purchased for preservation by the West Country Historic Omnibus and Transport Trust and returned to the mainland in August 2001.

Thomas Hardy, Lawrence of Arabia, and *Sir Christopher Wren* lined up outside the Pavilion Theatre, Weymouth, in May 1986 ready to be used in connection with the Borough's holiday publicity campaign. *Author*

VRT No. 559 ATA 559L *Henry Frier* stands in Easton Square whilst working a Portland Bill-Bowleaze Cove service on 6th June, 1999. At that time the open-tops were branded under the 'Southern Belle' logo and No. 559 carried an advert for Monkey World. *J.D. Ward*

Vintage Yellow Bus EDV 252D heading along Weymouth Esplanade on 29th May, 1997 with a Bowleaze Cove-King's Statue service whilst on hire to Southern National.

J.D. Ward

To supplement the original Ford Transit 16-seat minibuses various batches of new vehicles were acquired, together with some second-hand examples - including some from Southampton City Bus during 1990. Second-hand full size buses have also been purchased in recent years. In March 1998 three Leyland Nationals from Brighton Hove & District ran in their previous owner's livery until eventually repainted. In the same year new Dennis Darts arrived for use on the grant - assisted Weymouth-Axminster service, whilst vehicle shortages also caused the hiring of double-decks from Bournemouth Transport during 1998 and 1999. By 2000 many of the original Ford Transit vehicles of 1986 had been disposed of. They had given almost 14 years of service with very little trouble and although dismissively referred to as 'bread vans' had proved a good workhorse.

By the summer of 2001 of the 71 vehicles allocated to Weymouth there were only the VRT open-toppers remaining of the former Southern National fleet. The remainder consisted of 27 Mercedes Benz 709Ds, Carlyle B29F minibuses, 9 Dennis Dart, Plaxton N39F, 8 Volvo B6s, Wright N36F, 2 Leyland National B50F and 4 Leyland Lynx B49F single-decks, the latter formerly with First City Line (Bristol). The main double-deck allocation was eight Leyland Olympians, Roe B47/29F, transferred from First Badgerline, whilst the coach fleet consisted of two Volvo B10s, Plaxton C46F and six B10, Ikarus C53F vehicles, five of which were inherited from Bere Regis & District.

Three Mercedes-Benz 609D, Carlyle B29F minibuses in three different liveries lined up at the King's Statue during June 2001. Leading is No. 704, H909 WYB, in the revised 'former company' livery, centre an unidentified vehicle in the old Southern National yellow, black and orange mini-bus livery, and behind No. 720, J241 FYA, in advertising livery for Waterside Holiday Park.
Author

In the early days of Smith's bus service coaches were mainly employed, only one bus being owned. Lined up at Portland on 25th October 1982 from the left are: Bristol LH ECW B35F XPD 129M, former London County No. BN29; RLJ 292R a Bedford YMT, Plaxton C53F, acquired from Bluebird of Weymouth; UAA 355P a Bedford YMT, Duple C53F, previously with Buddens, of Woodfalls; and AAR 222K, a Bedford YRQ with Caetano C45F body obtained from Thomas of Chichester.
Author

However, constant changes are taking place within the fleet, and the days of a new vehicle arriving at Weymouth garage for 15 years or so are long gone. Vehicle transfers around the First Bus empire are now commonplace, and the vehicle allocation for the summer of 2001 is already history.

Smiths

Apart from the odd minibus, the fleet up until 1982 had consisted of Bedford coaches, some of which were used for bus work. Apart from the short stay of a Bristol LHS in February 1982, it was not until October 1987 that the first two Leyland Leopard Alexander B53F buses joined the fleet, to be followed by five Bristol chassis and a Leyland National. The most interesting purchases were the four Bristol REs, the full details of which and other full size buses are given in the table overleaf. Likewise the Leyland Leopard, Alexander-bodied buses had an interesting history, and later went on to serve in other parts of the Cawlett group.

Early in 1994 the fleet consisted of 10 vehicles - four REs, one LH bus, one Ford Transit minibus, a 21-seat DP vehicle and three coaches. In the spring of 1996 the four REs were sold to Anslow of Pontypool, but on the journey to the new owners AHT 206J (1613) suffered engine failure, being returned to Portland and excluded from the sale. She was later repaired, and remained as a spare and contract vehicle.

PUS 159W, a Leyland Leopard Alexander-bodied B53F bus purchased in October 1987 from North East Bus Services of Gateshead. Photographed at the King's Statue the following month, this robust vehicle passed to North Devon Red Bus in October 1990.   J.D. Ward

Smith's Bristol RELL YHY 596J commences the descent from the top of Portland on 27th May, 1995. New to Bristol Omnibus in April 1971, then passing through Badgerline, Badger Vectis, and Western National whose livery it retained upon purchase by Smith's in September 1990. It still had this livery when sold to Anslow of Pontypool in 1996.   *J.D. Ward*

Bristol RELL AHT 206J of Smith's fleet, still retaining its Western National livery, picks up at the Town Bridge, Weymouth, on 11th October, 1994. New in April 1971 to Bristol Omnibus Company, this vehicle passed through three other companies and a bus war at Poole before entering the Smith's fleet in September 1990. When withdrawn at the end of 1999 it was the last surviving RE in the area.   *J.D. Ward*

Around the same time the Leyland Optare B33F, C810 KBT was disposed of, the entire bus service becoming minibus operated, and three Freight Rover Sherpas with Carlyle B20F bodies, E96 OUH, E158 RNY, and F202 YKG, were acquired from Red & White in December 1995. Five Iveco Daily B20F vehicles - F593 OHT, F583 OOU, F599 PWS, F600 PWS, and F614 PWS - were obtained from City Line (Bristol), in 1996-7. At other times the fleet was topped up with vehicles from the parent company.

In the autumn of 1998 the RE was repainted in a plain all-over blue livery and retained principally for school contract work, but at the end of July 1999 it was pressed into fare stage work between Weymouth and Dorchester owing to vehicle shortages, thus becoming the last RE employed in the area. With the closure of Smith's operation in that September this vehicle was transferred to Dorchester and later sold. At an original cost of approximately £11,000 she had given good value in her 27 years' service.

Smiths of Portland Full-Size Buses 1982-1999

Reg No.	Chassis	No.	Body	Type	No.	Built	Acq.	Sold
XPD 129M	Bristol LHS	LHS 162	ECW	B35F	21377	1974	/82	
PUS 157W	Leyland Leop.	8030196	Alexander	B53F		1980	10/87	10/90
PUS 159W	Leyland Leop.	8030459	Alexander	B53F		1980	10/87	10/90
OSJ 610R	Leyland Leop.	7603324	Alexander	B53F		1976	b4/88	10/90
GPD 306N	Bristol LH6L	LHS 171	ECW	B35F	21386	2/75	3/90	1996
YHY 596J	Bristol RELL	1296	ECW	B50F	18337	4/71	9/90	1996
YHY 586J	Bristol RELL	1259	ECW	B50F	18327	4/71	11/90	1996
LHT 173L	Bristol RELL	1913	ECW	B50F	20148	6/73	11/90	1996
AHT 206J	Bristol RELL	1312	ECW	B50F	18383	4/71	11/90	1999
C810 KBT	Leyland R/line		Optare	B33F			5/95	5/96
BPL 493T	Leyland Nat.		Leyland	B41F		7/79	/95	1996

Previous Owners

XPD 129M New to London Country as No. B29.

PUS 157W North East Bus Services, Gateshead. New to Central Scottish No. T402. To Highland Scottish 1885 No. 1054.

PUS 159W North East Bus Services, Gateshead. New to Central Scottish No. T404. To Highland Scottish 1985 No. 1059.

OSJ 610R Rigby, Lathom. New to Western Scottish No. 610, to Clydeside Scottish 1985, No. 610.

GPD 306N Tyne & Wear Omnibus, Gateshead.

YHY 586J New to Bristol Omnibus No.1206. To Badgerline 1/1/86. To Badger-Vectis No. 44 10/87. To Western National No. 1615 1/88. To Southern National 8/90. To Smiths 11/90.

YHY 596J New to Bristol Omnibus No.1216. To Badgerline 1/1/86. To Badger-Vectis No. 45 10/87. To Western National No. 1614 1/88. To Southern National 8/90. To Smiths 9/90.

LHT 173L New to Bristol Omnibus No.1319. To Badgerline 1/1/86. To Badger-Vectis No. 58 10/87. To Western National No. 1616 1/88. To Southern National 6/90. To Smiths 11/90.

AHT 206J New to Bristol Omnibus No 1222. To Badgerline 1/1/86. To Badger-Vectis No. 46 10/87. To Western National No. 1613 1/88. To Southern National 6/90. To Smiths 9/90.

C810 KBT Ex-Circle Line, Gloucester.

BPL 493T New to London Country No. SNB 493, to Kentish Bus No. 478.

Disposals

PUS 157W Pearce Darch & Willcox.

PUS 159W North Devon No. 3514.

YHY 586J P. Anslow Pontypool. To Lloyd, New Inn 6/97 scrap.

YHY 596J P. Anslow, Pontypool

LHT 173L P. Anslow, Pontypool. To Lloyd, New Inn 6/97 scrap.

AHT 206J To First Southern National transferred to Dorchester, sold.

C 810 KBT To Houston Ramm (dealer).

Standing outside Smith's Victoria Square garage whilst working the 'Portland Islander Service' on 1st June, 1996 is Ford Transit B16F C333 GFJ. It had been acquired the previous month from North Devon Red Bus, to whom it was new in 1986 as fleet No. 412.   *J.D. Ward*

Standing outside Smith's garage on 3rd November, 1995 is D510 OTA - a 1986 Iveco Daily, Robin Hood DP21F minibus. New to North Devon Red Bus as No. 510 in December 1986, it was acquired by Smith's in September 1993. The window alongside the vehicle was the office of the pre-war Portland Express Service.   *Author*

Dorset Transit

The Dorset Transit fleet consisted of vehicles transferred from the main Southern National fleet. The service commenced in June 1996 with six Mercedes Benz 709Ds with Carlyle B29F bodies, H908/9/10/13/14/16 WYB, two Iveco Daily Dormobile B20F, F590 OHT, F588 OOU, (both originally Bristol City Line 7590/88) and Ford Transit B16F C955 GYD. The only big bus in the Transit fleet was Leyland National (formerly Southern National) No. 2882, FDV 778V, which looked very smart in the Dorset Transit livery. During the August of both 1996 and 1997 two Bedfords of Dorchester Coachways were hired, TKM 108X and TKM 111X, these being high capacity 60 seaters (3-2 seating towards the rear) with capacity for 20 standing. These unusual buses had previously operated with Chalkwell of Westerham, Kent. Transit also frequently hired double-decks from Southern National. There were two unusual hirings, firstly a Damory Coaches of Blandford, Metrorider (F370 URU) with automatic transmission, which was exchanged for a conventional vehicle early in 1997 and employed on the Park Mead Road route. This allowed driver Keith Drummond, who had recently undergone a hip replacement, to return to work, and secondly a former Bristol Omnibus open-top K5G No. 8583, GHT 127, on 31st May, 1997 to celebrate the first year of Transit operation.

With the integration of the fleets following the 'First Bus' takeover there was no need for separate fleets, and with the introduction of the Volvo/Wright-bodied B36F vehicles Nos. 1802-1809, V802-809 EFB, in November 1999, the Transit mini-buses reverted to the Southern National fleet to replace some of the Ford Transits, thus bringing the story of this short-lived fleet to a close.

Resplendent in its new livery of white, orange and grey is A916 WYB - a 1991 Mercedes-Benz with Carlyle B29F body, formerly No. 710 in the Southern National fleet. Photographed here departing from Easton Square for Southwell on Saturday 1st June, 1996, the first day of operation of Portland services by Dorset Transit. *J.D. Ward*

The only 'big bus' in the Dorset Transit fleet, Leyland National FDV 778V, stands at Portland Bill. Formerly No. 2882 in the Southern National fleet, it was later painted in the Atlantic Blue livery of dedicated vehicles operating the Barnstaple-Bideford-Westward Ho! route of North Devon Red Bus, arriving at Weymouth in that livery. The repaint into white, orange, and grey suited it well.   *Henry Frier*

The first two full size buses acquired by Weybus were former Blackpool Corporation AEC Swift, Marshall B47D single-decks. OFR 971M, repainted in a black and white livery, passes Wyke Hotel whilst operating a 'Seaside Shuttle' between Chesil Beach Holiday Camp and the King's Statue in September 1988.   *Author*

Weybus

Despite the other difficulties, the Weybus fleet was well maintained and few faults could be found that any vehicle examiner would not have discovered even with a top class major company. Early vehicles were a mixture of mini, full size buses and coaches, often appearing painted black and white. Early large vehicles of note were two former Blackpool Corporation AEC Swifts OFR 971/89M, which appeared during 1988, but the following year an ex-East Kent AEC Swift, RJG 206G, two Alexander-bodied C49F coaches, RAG 294M and SCS 329M, and a former Doncaster Corporation Seddon Pennine 4 DP25F bus, TDT 624L, put in an appearance.

There were plans in 1995 to introduce open-top ex-London Routemasters, going as far as to illustrate them on the timetable, but the scheme did not proceed and Weymouth was denied the famous London bus. Once established the fleet relied heavily on the Freight Rover Sherpa mini-bus, many with Carlyle B18F bodies and mostly purchased from Red & White whose basic livery they retained, which with the Weybus fleet name applied, looked well turned-out.

It was almost cash bags at 10 paces! Two Weybus and two Southern National buses await passengers during the off peak period of the afternoon at Littlemoor estate on 1st November, 1994.   *Author*

In a show of solidarity, five Weybus vehicles line up at the King's Statue in August 1995. The first two are D463 CKV and D470 CKV, both Freight Rover Sherpas. The adopted Red & White livery and simple fleet name made the fleet attractive.   *Author*

Weybus Freight Rover Sherpa, Carlyle B16F, F234 BAX, stands in Easton Square on 4th November, 1985. New to Red & White in 1989 and acquired by Weybus in 1994.   *J.D. Ward*

Barry's 'Interbus' RHG 319K, a Seddon Pennine B46F formerly Burnley & Pendle Corporation No. 119, stands at Manor Park, Dorchester on 28th June, 1982 whilst working the Dorchester town service. *Author*

Barry's and Bluebird

The Barry's Coach fleet mostly consisted of second-hand vehicles over the years, the only ones within the scope of this work being the four Seddon/Pennine B46F single-deck buses purchased in 1982 for the Dorchester Town service from Burnley & Pendle Corporation: RHG 315/6/8/9K, fleet Nos. 115/6/8/9, two Bristol REs, DRX 625K, former Alder Valley No. 474, and HTD 323K, Blackburn Corporation No. 173.

The Bluebird fleet is also beyond the scope of this work except for the fact that several Bristol RE buses have been used over the years for school contracts. Where Volume Three of *Isle of Portland Railways* left off the Bedford was the dominant vehicle in the fleet, but today only one remains and of the present fleet of 23 vehicles 11 are Volvo, reflecting the high quality of tours (both English and continental) and private hire work that this company, now in its 77th year, operates.

Ticket Issuing Systems

The Speed Setright ticket machine, which had been a faithful servant for the past 30 years, was replaced in October 1983 by the Timtronic, a computerised ticket issuing and data collection system. However, in the fast moving world of electronics, this was replaced 10 years later by the Wayfarer II, to be followed by the Wayfarer III, also used when Dorset Transit commenced operations. Smiths had used the Speed Setright, until later years when they changed over to the Waysaver, a version of the Wayfarer II without a module. Both Weybus and Barry's had always used the Speed Setright.

Bus Preservation

The arrival of new diesel-powered vehicles into the Southern National fleet during 1937 allowed five of the still fairly new petrol engine double-decks to be withdrawn, including No. 2849, DR 4902 - a 1929 Leyland Titan with a Leyland L27/24ROS body. Formerly a North Devon-based vehicle it worked at Weymouth during the summer of 1936, and was sold for £59 to Chivers Jams for staff transport. Photographed at the former Clapham Transport Museum, it incorrectly displays the livery of the Eastern Counties Omnibus Company. This fine example of an all-Leyland bus still with its original body and open staircase, is now in the care of the Science Museum. *D.M. Habgood*

For 10 years the Dorset Transport Circle organised the annual Weymouth Bus Rally with a road run that included a circuit of Portland. Thus on the first Sunday in July preserved buses and coaches from as far afield as Liverpool and Yorkshire could be seen together on the island. During the first rally in 1971 a Provincial AEC double-deck, Burton-on-Trent Guy single-deck, a Birkenhead Corporation Guy double-deck and a Southern National Dennis Mace line up at Southwell. At its peak almost 100 vehicles took part in this spectacular event. *C.L. Caddy*